THE COMPLETE GUIDE TO
CAT
BREEDS

Bounty
Books

AN OCEANA BOOK

This edition published in 2005 by
Bounty Books, a division of
Octopus Publishing Group Ltd
2-4 Heron Quays
London E14 4JP

ISBN 0 7537 1240 7
ISBN13 9780753712405

QUMTIE3

This book is produced by
Quantum Publishing Ltd.
6 Blundell Street
London N7 9BH

Manufactured in Singapore by
Pica Digital Pte. Ltd.
Printed in China by
CT Printing Ltd

THE COMPLETE GUIDE TO

E S

CONTENTS

EVOLUTION AND HISTORY

Persians have the look and feel of elegance and fine living. The Norwegian Forest Cat is reminiscent of the wild, untamed world. The Ragdoll is an adorable, docile animal, and the Siamese exudes the world of the mystical. As different as they are, these four of the hundred-plus breeds of domestic cat that exist in the world today are all descendants of the same ancestor.

A weasel-like creature called *Miacis* lived on Earth in the Eocene period of 50 million years ago. From this fierce, successful creature evolved countless generations of carnivores. We can recognize in those early creatures the forebears of our domestic cats, and identify the same survival skills.

Felidae is the family name for all cats, and is divided into three genera: *Panthera*, which includes big cats such as lions and tigers that have a small hyoid bone at the base of their tongue; *Acinonyx*, represented only by the cheetah, which has claws that cannot fully retract; and *Felis*, which includes smaller cats such as the domestic cat that have a rigid hyoid bone and cannot roar. The domestic cat, *Felis catus*, is probably descended from two species: *F. sylvestris* (European Wildcat) and *F. libyca* (African Wildcat).

As any pair of domestic cats, from anywhere in the world, will readily interbreed, it means that they are of a single species, descended from a common ancestor.

Domestication of the cat probably first took place in the Middle East, and the cats encouraged to approach people were almost certainly *Felis lybica*, the African wild cat. This is a lithe animal, very similar to a domestic tabby in colour. Many of the skulls from Ancient Egyptian cat cemeteries resemble *Felis lybica*, while a small proportion are of cats resembling the jungle cat, *Felis chaus*. It would appear that the Ancient Egyptians tamed both types, but the African wild cat was easily the more popular, and probably more amenable to domestication.

Egypt was the greatest corn-growing area of the ancient world, and huge granaries were constructed to store the grain from good harvests for use in leaner years. As rodent controllers, cats must have been vital to the economy of those times. The Ancient Egyptians also appreciated the natural link between the cat and the lion, and worshipped the goddess Bast, also called Pasht or Oubasted, who first appeared with the head of a lion, and later with the head of a cat. Bast was seen as a goddess of love, and of the moon. The cat was connected with her as love-goddess because of the animal's natural fecundity, and as moon-goddess because of the varying shape of the pupils of the cat's eyes, which were thought to enlarge and contract with the waxing and waning of the moon. Egyptian statues of Bast show her connection with fertility and pleasure. In several statues she stands upright, an alert cat's head surmounting a figure holding a sistrum in one hand and a rattle in the other. The rattle symbolized both phallus and womb, and the symbolic fertility of the goddess was further reinforced by several kittens, normally five, sitting at her feet. Women of the period often wore fertility amulets depicting Bast and her feline family.

The original Egyptian name of the cat was mau, perhaps from its call of 'miaow', which also meant 'to see'. The Egyptians considered the cat's unblinking gaze gave it powers to seek out truth and to see into the afterlife. Bast was sometimes called the Lady of Truth, and was used in mummification ceremonies to ensure life after death.

Cats played such a complex and important part in the lives of the Ancient Egyptians that the living animals were pampered and in some cases worshipped. After the death of a cat, whole families would go into mourning, and the cat's body was embalmed and placed in a sacred vault. Thousands of mummified cats have been discovered in Egypt, some so well preserved that they have added to our store of knowledge of the earliest domesticated cats.

The custom of keeping cats spread slowly throughout the Middle Eastern countries. A Sanskrit document of 1000 BC mentions a pet cat, and the Indian epics *Ramayana* and *Mahabharata*, of about 500 BC, both contain stories about cats. The Indians at that time worshipped a feline goddess of maternity called Sasti, and for decades Hindus were obliged to take responsibility for feeding at least one cat. Cats reached China around AD 400, and in AD 595 an empress was recorded as having been bewitched by a cat spirit. By the 12th century AD rich Chinese families kept yellow and white cats known as 'lion-cats', which were highly valued as pets. Vermin control was undertaken by longhaired cats, and cats were traded in street markets. Pet cats were introduced into Japan from China in the reign of Emperor Ichi-Jo who lived from AD 986 to 1011. It is recorded that on the tenth day of the fifth moon the emperor's white cat gave birth to five white kittens, and a nurse was appointed to see that they were brought up as carefully as royal princes. Many legends and stories of cats survive in Japanese literature, the most enduring image being that of the *Maneki-neko*, the listening or beckoning cat, which is still to be found in ornaments and amulets today.

Throughout the world, prior to the witch-hunts of the Middle Ages, cats were treated with affection and respect. Their greatest attribute was their efficiency in controlling vermin.

Gods of one religion may become the demons of its successor, and in the case of the cat, its nocturnal habits, independence, sense of self-preservation and often erotic behaviour accelerated the process during the 16th and 17th centuries. Witch-hunting then reached its climax, and cats figured prominently in

Left *The beckoning cat provides an example of the dual role of charms and amulets to attract good fortune and to ward off evil.*

most witch trials throughout Europe. Even as late as the 19th century Basque farmers claimed that witches appeared as black cats and were greatly feared.

Eventually the cat's fortunes turned once more. They became prized possessions, and those with unusual colours and markings were favoured as pets. They were carried between the world's continents as precious gifts, and gave rise to the many breeds and varieties that we know today.

In the 17th century, cats of the traditional tabby pattern were taken by the Pilgrims to America. (Today, almost half the cats in the Boston area have that same tabby pattern, and the ranges of the original toms can be determined by cats with coats of that pattern). By the 18th century, they were again common in households.

The concept of breeds began in the mid-19th century, and by the end of the century, early pedigree breeds were exhibited at the first cat shows.

Descent of the modern cat

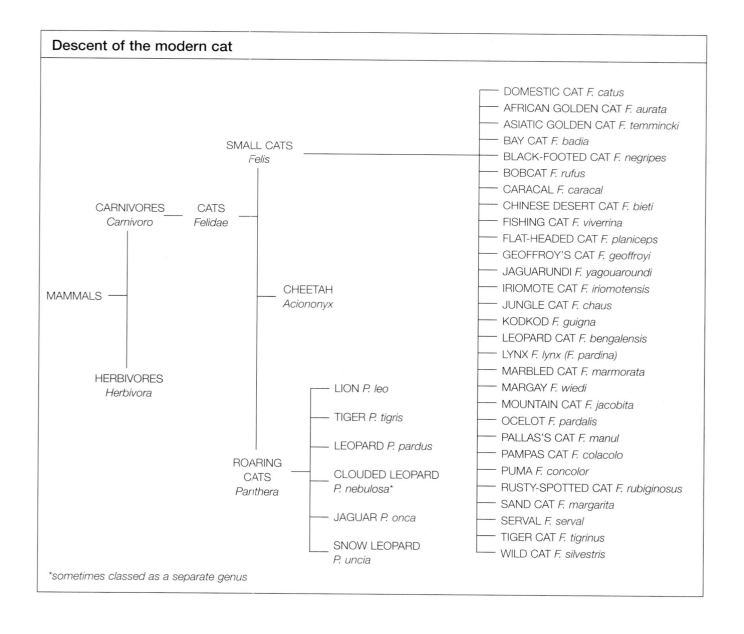

*sometimes classed as a separate genus

DISTANT COUSINS

Cats of one sort or another have been around for 50 million years, long before man made his first fumbling appearance on earth. The first of the long line leading to the tabby curled up at the foot of your bed was a weasel-like carnivore called Miacis *(left). It had a long body and short legs and, in addition to being the predecessor of the cat, was probably the grand-daddy of the dog and the bear as well.*

It took another 10 million years for the first cat-like carnivore to appear (and yet another 10 million before the dog made its bow). This first cat is known as *Dinictis* and was about the same size as the lynx. It looked very much like the modern cat. However, although its canine teeth were larger, its brain was considerably smaller.

Over the next 10 million years or so, *Dinictis* appears to have split itself into two groups. One of these included the family *Felidae*, to which all cats – domestic, wild, lions, tigers, etc. – belong. In addition to these, *Dinictis* also includes the civet, the genet, and the snake-killing mongoose, all of whom are cousins of the domestic cat.

The second group included the great sabre-toothed cat, which roamed the plateaux and forest regions of their prehistoric times.

The North American species, *Smilodon californicus*, was one of the most advanced sabre-tooths, and its remains have been found in great numbers at the

Above *Today's cats are divided into three genera, one of which is the Panthera. The lion falls into this group of the great cats.*

Left *Another of the genera is the Acinonyx. In this group is the cheetah which has claws that cannot be fully retracted.*

asphalt pits at Rancho La Brea, near Los Angeles, Southern California. Many examples of prehistoric big cats have been recovered from this area. Millions of years ago there were pools of water lying on top of the tar pools. Many animals which came to drink were trapped in the tar, and their bones were preserved in the asphalt.

Also found at Rancho La Brea, although in much smaller numbers, are the remains of *Felis atrox*, the American Lion. Perhaps fewer of them were trapped because they were too intelligent to be caught in this fashion. This animal was a near relation of the European Cave Lion, which was still around in the fifth century BC. Indeed, some of them are reputed to have attacked Xerxes and his army as they invaded Macedonia.

The last of the Californian line lived about 13,000 years ago. Sabre-tooths were extinct in Europe long before this. These creatures were adapted to hunt the thick-skinned mammoths and mastodons. When these giant land mammals disappeared from the face of the earth, such highly-specialized predators as the sabre-tooth went with them. It is from *Felidae*, the more adaptable descendants of *Dinictis*, that the 34 species of cat known to modern man have developed.

The sole exception to this is the cheetah, which belongs in a genus of its own.

These 21st-century members of the family have adapted and diversified to meet the wide range of climate and environment they are likely to find. They are all carnivores and highly efficient hunters. Some prefer the solitary life on the prowl, while others (the lion is a notable example) like to live and hunt in groups.

Similarities between *Felis sylvestris*, the modern European or Scottish Wild Cat and the modern house cat, are so obvious that it seems highly probable that the Wild Cat, now extinct outside Europe and Asia, was the last stop on the evolutionary train before arriving at the cuddly creature purring in front of the fire. The Wild Cat hunts small mammals like rabbits and hares, but because it sometimes attacks poultry it is being gradually destroyed in Europe.

The evolution of the cat

Dinictis About 50 million years ago, this carnivorous cat-like mammal, ancestor of the cats, inhabited the earth.

Pseudaelurus Until about 25 million years ago, this relatively long-legged mammal had evolved with more cat-like features.

Felis lunensis Among several species of wild cat that evolved, and lived until about 12 million years ago, was Martelli's wildcat.

Felidae Today's cats, large and small. Highly developed and efficient carnivores, designed for hunting and killing.

SPREAD OF THE DOMESTIC CAT

The fact that domestic cats have been systematically bred for only about one hundred years makes it difficult to ascertain the origins of certain key factors in their make-up.

The stocky body type found in the Persians and various Shorthairs points to the possible influence of the European wild cat in their ancestry, whereas the light-boned and slender 'foreign' cats, such as the Abyssinian, have bodies similar to that exhibited by the African Wild Cat. In Asia, lightboned cats have been known for centuries and isolated gene pools aided the standardization of specific colours and coat patterns. Very few mutations affecting the original wild type conformation, coat length, colour and pattern have been necessary to provide the ingredients from which all of today cats have been bred.

1 Manx
The Isle of Man, midway between England and Ireland, is generally agreed to be the homeland and birthplace of the Manx.

2 Rex
The first Cornish Rex, its curled coat caused by the action of a mutant gene, was discovered in a litter of kittens in 1950.

3 Chinchilla
The Chinchilla was man-made by crossing cats of various colours with Silver Tabby Persians in England in the late 1800s.

4 Abyssinian
In the 1880s, such cats were taken from Ethiopia by servicemen returning to Britain at the end of the Abyssinian War.

5 Siamese
First brought to England from Thailand in the 1880s, the first Siamese are said to have been prized by the Thai royal family.

6 Burmese
A cat called Wong Mau *was taken from Burma to the United States in 1930, and was the foundation queen of the breed.*

7 Birman
At the end of World War II, a pair of temple cats was sent to France, and from these the breed was established.

8 Russian Blue
Shorthaired blue cats are said to have been brought from the port of Archangel, in Russia, and were called Russian Blue.

North America

1

2

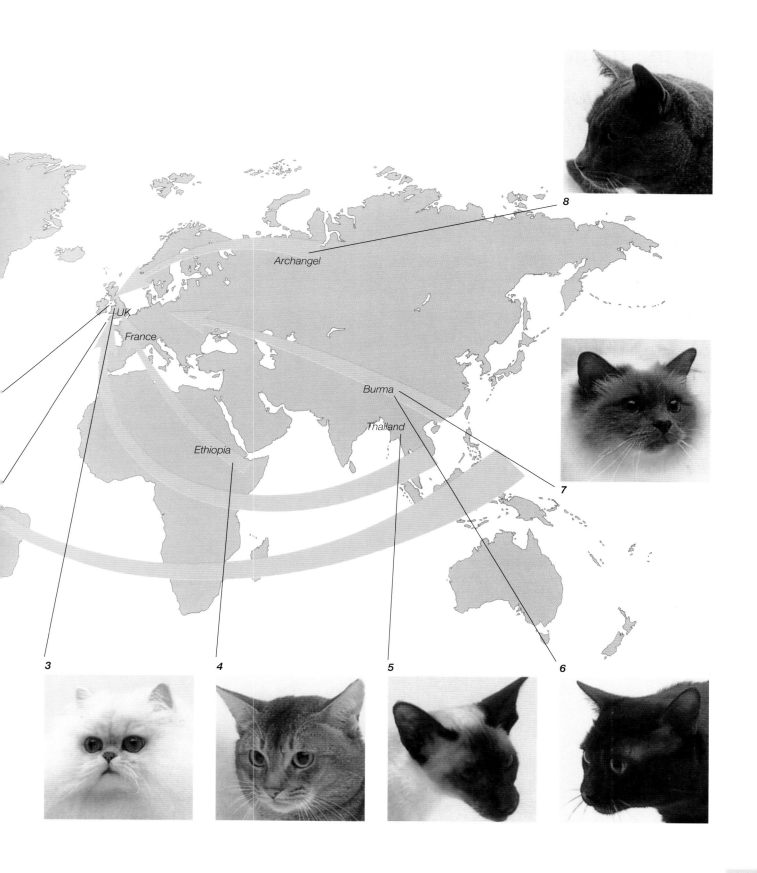

Archangel

UK

France

Burma

Thailand

Ethiopia

8

7

3

4

5

6

BODY SHAPE

For over a century, cat fanciers have tried, using various techniques, to manipulate the conformation, coat colours and patterns of their favourite varieties of the domestic cat. By carefully controlled selective breeding, they have endeavoured to create new varieties and even entirely new breeds.

In general shape and overall size, all breeds of domestic cats have retained the same basic structure as their ancestors, unlike dogs, which have been selectively bred to produce very wide ranges of shape and height. Cats are therefore free from many of the skeletal abnormalities that can affect dogs. Some defects are occasionally encountered: these include shortened, bent or kinked tails, cleft palates, flattened chests and polydactylism (extra toes). In the main, evolution seems to have been particularly kind in designing the cat, proceeding along such a well-ordered path of natural selection that it remains an efficient and perfect carnivore of convenient size, still well capable of hunting and killing small animals and birds. The cat's frame permits fluid, co-ordinated and graceful movements at all speeds. Its taut-muscled body and legs enable it to make impressive leaps and bounds. The retractile nature of the sharp claws allows fast sprinting over short distances, holding and gripping of prey, and fast climbing of convenient trees when danger threatens. The cat's brain is large and well developed, enabling it to rapidly assimilate facts and react quickly. Its adaptable eyes can cope with extreme lighting conditions, allowing perfect vision in both bright sunlight and dim twilight. The mobile ears work to catch the faintest sound, and the sensitive nose, allied to the perceptive Jacobson's organ in the mouth, can identify the faintest of scents imperceptible to humans.

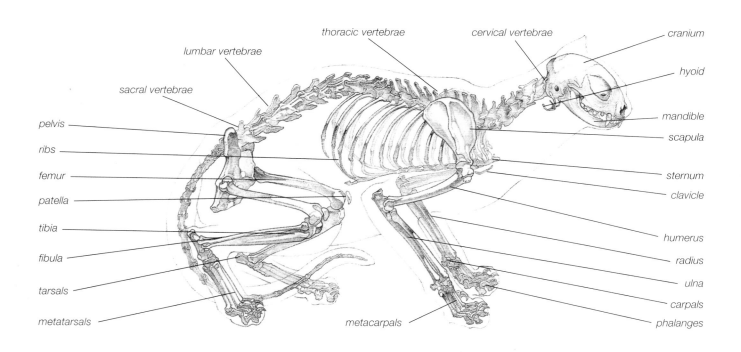

thoracic vertebrae — cervical vertebrae — cranium

lumbar vertebrae

sacral vertebrae

hyoid

pelvis

mandible

ribs

scapula

femur

sternum

patella

clavicle

tibia

fibula

humerus

tarsals

radius

ulna

metatarsals

carpals

metacarpals

phalanges

Pedigree breeds of domestic cats have been developed to fit certain standards of conformation, colour and coat pattern. This has been done over many generations, with dedicated breeders working out exactly what the desired feline end-product would look like, and setting out to achieve it with careful and selective breeding. Today there are two main types of pedigree cat: those with chunky, heavyweight bodies and large round heads, and a lighter, finer type with lighter bones and a longer head.

Cats of the heavier type come in a wide range of colours and coat patterns, and may be longhaired or shorthaired. The former include Persians and similar breeds; while the shorthairs cover cats such as the British, American, European and Exotic Shorthairs.

Below The cat is the perfect predator, and built for a combination of speed and coordination. Its skeleton consists of a highly evolved framework of efficient levers, connected by powerful muscles. Massive muscles in the hindquarters enable the cat to propel itself forward in short bursts of speed.

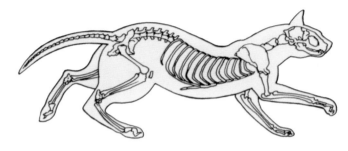

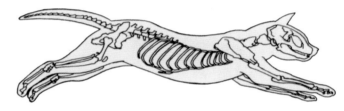

Right Cats keep their muscles in trim at all times. The awakening cat yawns and stretches, first the spine, tail and forelegs, then the hips and the hindlegs.

Lightweight cats are more variable in their characteristics. The Orientals, including the distinctive Siamese, are at the furthest extreme from the heavier types, with very fine bones, very long bodies, legs and tails, long wedge-shaped heads and large ears. Less extreme are the Foreign Shorthairs and Rex cats, each variety having its own very recognizable features.

Some breeds have arisen from mixtures of heavy and lightweight types; these have intermediate features.

SIGHT, TASTE AND SMELL

A cat's eyes differ from ours in several ways. They observe less of the colour spectrum, having fewer cones, but more rod sensors allowing the perception of more brightness in dim light. The iris of the cat's eye opens and closes to a greater extent and the eyeball is more spherical and, in relation to body size, very much larger than in the human.

Although it is said that cats can see in the dark, this is not true, though the feline pupils are able to expand widely, giving excellent vision in very dim light conditions. The pupil is contracted and expanded by an intricate web of muscles set in a figure-of-eight configuration in the iris. Within the eye light is reflected off the tapetum lucidium which has a photomultiplying effect on the light admitted.

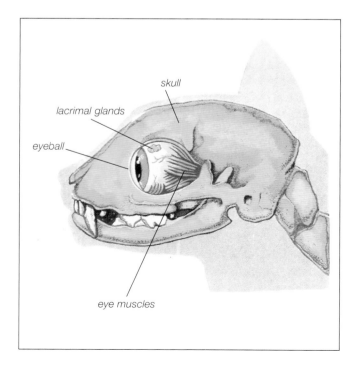

skull

lacrimal glands

eyeball

eye muscles

Vision

Humans may have better daylight vision than cats, but as dusk falls the cat scores, for although it cannot see in total darkness, its unusual pupils are able to expand to give excellent vision in very dim conditions.

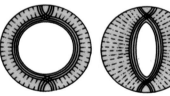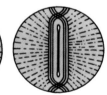

1 Changes in the size and shape of the pupil generally relate to the amount of light entering the eye. In darkness the pupil dilates.
2 In natural diffused daylight the pupil is seen a normal vertical oval shape.
3 In natural light, when the cat is relaxed, the pupil closes down to a narrow slit.

***Left** The cat's eye is set in a bony socket in the skull, cushioned by pads of fat and connected by muscles, enabling it to move in various directions. Lacrimal glands provide tears to wash the eye.*

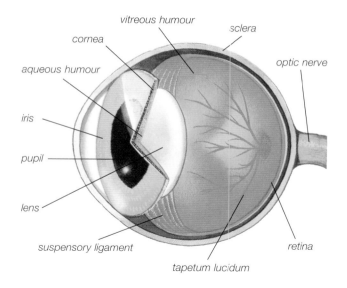

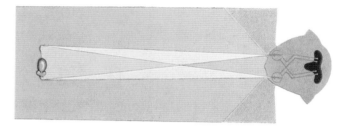

Above Both eyes face forward allowing the fields of vision to overlap. This produces stereoscopic sight and enables the hunting cat accurate assessment of distance and prey location.

Left The slightly egg-shaped eye is surrounded by the tough sclera, replaced at the front by the transparent cornea, behind which the aqueous humour protects the iris and pupil. Jellylike vitreous humour fills the cavity behind the lens, and at the back of the eye is the light sensitive retina, and the reflective tapetum lucidum. The optic nerve transmits signals from the eye to the brain.

Taste and smell

Smell is the most important of its senses to the cat. Smell is closely linked to taste since the nasal passage opens into the mouth. As well as assisting its hunting pursuits, smell is an essential part of the cat's sexual life. The vomeronasal or Jacobson's organ in the roof of its mouth enables the cat to identify minute particles of scent.

Flehmen Reaction This is exhibited when the cat is confronted by chemicals in smells, either of sexual origin or from musky odours. Airborne molecules are trapped on the tongue which is flicked back to press on the opening of the Jacobson's organ. Information is relayed to the brain's hypothalmus, which dictates the cat's response.

Below The cat exhibiting the flehmen reaction stretches its neck, opens its mouth and curls back its upper lips in a snarl. It may be so affected by a smell that it also starts salivating.

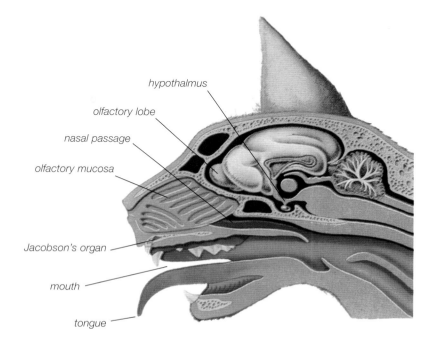

HEARING

This sense is highly developed in the cat and registers two octaves higher than the human ear. The comparatively large and mobile ears of the ordinary domestic cat enable it to flex them sideways and backwards in order to pinpoint the source of very slight sounds – important to a natural crepuscular predator.

Anatomy of the ear

Sound waves are funnelled down the external auditory canal to the ear drum. In the middle ear, weak vibrations are turned into stronger vibrations. Nerve signals are then sent along the auditory nerve to the brain.

Above *Even when apparently occupied, cats are alert to sounds around them.*

Right *The anatomy of the ear.*

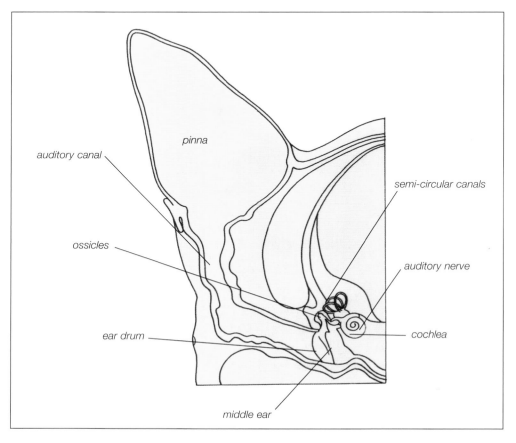

pinna

auditory canal

semi-circular canals

ossicles

auditory nerve

cochlea

ear drum

middle ear

CLAWS AND BODY TYPE

Claws

The domestic cat has retractile claws which are normally sheathed, allowing the animal silent footfalls. When required for grasping prey, defensive measures or climbing, the claws are extended by muscles tightening the tendons.

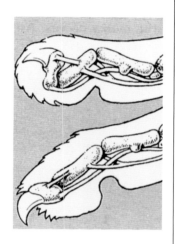

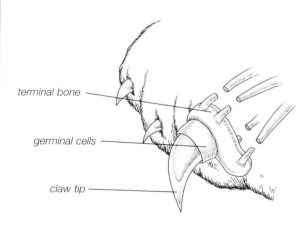

terminal bone

germinal cells

claw tip

Declawing Onychectomy is an operation involving the surgical removal of a cat's claws, normally performed only on the forepaws. Illegal in Britain and not generally advised by the US veterinary profession, the declawing process removes the claw and the germinal cells responsible for its regrowth as well as all or part of the terminal bone of the toe. Declawed cats are deprived of their prime form of defence and therefore should never be allowed out of the home.

Body types

The Longhair or Persian body type is large boned and stocky.

The Shorthair breeds are similar in structure to Persians.

Foreign and Oriental cats are fine-boned and dainty.

Most cat breeds with heavy conformation, such as the Persian and the Shorthair, have large round heads, with large round eyes set wide apart above a short snub nose on a broad face. The ears are small but have a wide base, and are placed far apart on the head, complementing the rounded appearance of the skull.

Cats of light conformation, such as the Oriental and Foreign Shorthairs, have longer heads of various shapes, and the eye shape varies for each specific breed. Long-coated cats with light conformation have various head and eye shapes, according to the standards laid down by their breed associations.

The head of the Longhair or Persian is typically round, with round eyes and full cheeks. The tiny ears are set wide apart.

The head of the Shorthair is similar in shape to that of the Persian when viewed from the front only.

Foreign and Oriental cats have long narrow heads and large ears. Head shape varies in the individual breeds.

In profile the Persian's head is rather flat. The short snub nose shows a definite 'break' at eyelevel.

The profile of a typical Shorthair breed is less flat than that of the Persian with a short, broad nose.

Oriental cats have long, almost Roman noses with no 'break' at eyelevel and a flat forehead.

Below *One of the primary characteristics that distinguish one breed from another is eye shape. The three basic shapes are almond, slanted and round. Many cats' eyes are of an intermediate shape between these three types.*

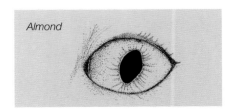

Almond

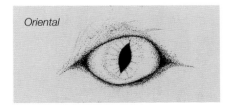

Oriental

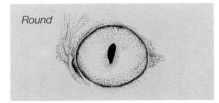

Round

EYES

Colours of eyes

Each breed and variety of cat has a permitted eye colour or a range of colours, as set down by the governing cat organizations. The pupil is generally black; the coloured area is called the iris. Irises may even vary in colour within an individual cat, as is the case with Odd-Eyed Whites.

While cats' eyes come in a rainbow of different colours – greens, blues, golds – colour is not at all important to cats. Tests have shown that cats can distinguish between various colours, but they don't really need to be aware of them. Being able to detect movement is much more important.

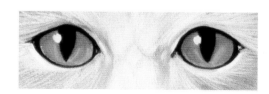

COAT TYPES

Pedigree cats have a diverse range of coat types ranging from the full and profuse pelt of the Persian to the very fine sleek and close-lying coats of the Siamese and Orientals. Between the two extremes are the long, soft and silky coats of the longhaired foreign breeds and the thick, dense coats of some of the shorthaired varieties. Some breeds should have 'double' coats, with a thick woolly undercoat and a longer, sleeker top coat. The Cornish Rex has a coat devoid of guard hairs, and naturally curled awn and down hairs. The Devon Rex has modified guard, awn and down hairs which produce a waxy effect. The Sphynx or Canadian Hairless cat is at the extreme end of the coat-type range, being merely covered in some parts with a fine down.

Persian
Long, soft coat with profuse down hairs nearly as long as the guard hairs, producing a typically long and full coat.

Maine Coon
Long silky coat, heavier and less uniform than that of the Persian due to less uniform and denser down hairs.

Shorthair
Shorthair coats are very variable, ranging from the British and American breeds to the foreigns.

Sphynx
Apparently hairless, the Sphynx does have a light covering of down hairs on some areas of the body.

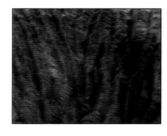

Cornish Rex
The tightly curled coat of the Cornish Rex is caused by the absence of guard hairs and short awn hairs.

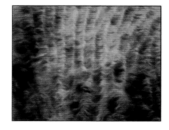

Devon Rex
Genetically modified guard and awn hairs in this breed closely resemble down hairs.

American Wirehair
Quite different to the two rex coats the wirehair has crimped awn hairs and waved guard hairs.

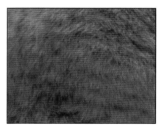

Oriental
In the Siamese and Oriental cats, the coat is short, fine and close-lying, quite different from other cats.

Coat Colours and Patterns

The natural colour of the domestic cat is tabby, which may be one of four basic patterns. The wild type is ticked tabby or agouti, and the other tabby patterns are mackerel (striped), spotted and classic (marbled or blotched). The pigment melanin produces black hairs, and most of the self-coloured coats seen in cats are produced by modification of this pigment, or by the way in which it is distributed in the individual hair fibres.

Types of Tipping

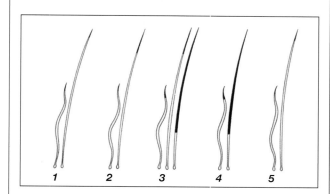

In the unusually coloured tipped, shaded and smoke breeds, each effect is produced by a proportion of each hair having a coloured tip while the rest of the hair is of a paler colour.

1. Tipped cats such as the British Tipped or Chinchilla have tipping at the very ends of the hairs, producing a sparkling effect.
2. Tipping extending further down the hair shaft produces the more strongly coloured varieties.
3. Variable bands of colour in different areas of the coat give rise to tabby effects.
4. Tipping extending almost to the white hair roots produces the smoke coat in many breeds.
5. In golden varieties, the white base coat of the silver varieties is replaced by a tawny yellow colour.

Solids

Cats of self- or solid-coloured breeds must be of a single, solid colour throughout with no pattern, shading, ticking or other variation in colour. These are the most common solid colours.

Black

Blue

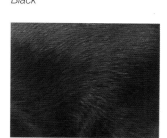

Chocolate

Lilac

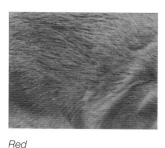

Red

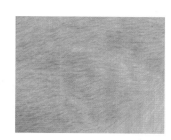

Cream

Cinnamon

White

Tabby Markings

There are four varieties of tabby patterns each can be found in any of the tabby colours.

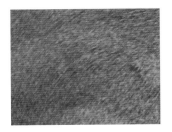

Ticked

Mackerel

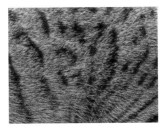

Spotted

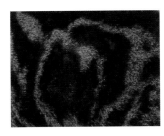

Classic

Tabby Colours

Tabbies are found in a wide range of colours.
Here is a selection.

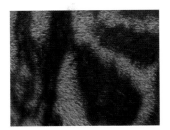

Brown

Blue

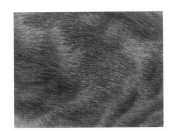

Chocolate

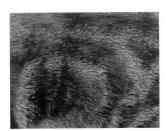

Brown Patched

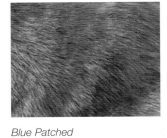

Blue Patched

Red

Silver

Abyssinian

Abyssinian cats have coats which are gently shaded;
each hair is lighter at the root and darker at the tip.

Usual

Blue

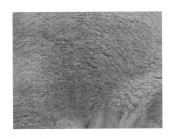

Sorrel

Fawn

Coloured Tips

Coats of this sort, with the hairs darkening in varying degrees towards the roots, are found in a number of colours, some of which are shown here.

Black Smoke

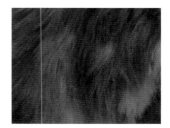

Blue Smoke

Chocolate Smoke

Lilac Smoke

Chinchilla Silver

Chinchilla Golden

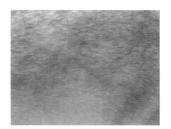

Black Tipped Silver

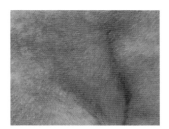

Blue Tipped Silver

Himalayan

Cats with the Himalayan coat pattern, such as the Siamese, have pale coats with the main colour restricted to the head and extremities.

Seal Point

Blue Point

Red Point

Cream Point

Lilac Point

Chocolate Point

Seal Tabby

Red Tabby Point

Tonkinese

Tonkinese cats, which are light-phase Burmese cats, show a modified 'pointed' effect. The coats are darker than those of cats with true Himalayan colouring, so the 'points' are not so dramatic.

Brown   *Lilac*   *Chocolate*   *Red*

Cream   *Lilac Tortie*   *Blue Tortie*   *Tabby*

Multiple Colours

As every cat lover knows, cats come in coats of many colours apart from those already described, most of which are recognized for show purposes in one breed or another. The tortoiseshells are the most common, but there are endless varieties, including the unusual Mi-ke pattern of the Japanese Bobtail.

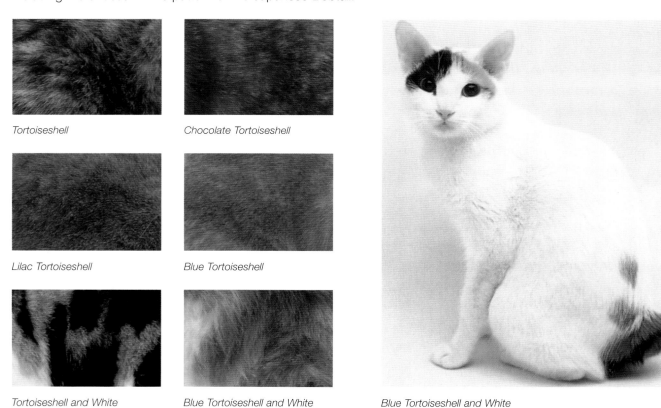

Tortoiseshell   *Chocolate Tortoiseshell*

Lilac Tortoiseshell   *Blue Tortoiseshell*

Tortoiseshell and White   *Blue Tortoiseshell and White*   *Blue Tortoiseshell and White*

A BALANCED VIEW

Cats have a deserved reputation as sure-footed creatures, and yet some will not even attempt a walk along a narrow ledge, fence or the top of a wall. Kittens may attempt an exploratory step or two, but then reverse to safety. One can, therefore, conclude that such ventures are the result of maturity, and that the confidence to attempt them is tied to experience.

Just like humans, cats are subject to hazards and infirmities. They get pregnant, they become arthritic, they grow old and less agile. There are also the tragic cases of disability caused by man's interference. Many additives and pesticides can cause damage to the central nervous system and send the poor creature toppling from the simplest perch.

How does a cat halfway across a 'tightrope' retrace its steps? If the area on which it is balancing is sufficiently wide, it will balance on its hind legs, then transfer the weight to one front leg, which is placed as far back between the hind ones as possible. The next step is to bring the other front leg around to carry the weight, while it shifts its hind quarters.

If, however, the cat falls, it may slow its descent by hanging on with its claws. One of the signs of this sort of feline trauma is that the claws are scraped down to their bleeding quicks. If a cat knows that there are obstructions below, it will always try to leap clear. However, an uncalculated fall from any height may upset the animal's reactions. A drop from a considerable height may result in serious injury, no matter how fit or prepared the cat may be.

Occasionally, legs are broken, but more often than not these powerful and resilient limbs absorb the impact with little more than a slight strain. However, the relatively large head of the cat is quite likely to hit the ground, and this can often mean a fractured jaw, or damage to the roof of the mouth.

It is possible to damage the cat's sense of balance through excessive doses of some drugs. The mature cat affected in this way may never get used to the idea that a skill it once practised with a flourish now completely escapes it. It will go on trying to balance on ledges only to find that it is back where it started on the ground.

The self-righting reflex

The famous feline attribute of always being able to land on its feet is not wholly accurate, but a falling cat is often able to reposition its body during falling to avoid serious injury on landing. A set of information which reaches the brain from the eyes is combined with impulses from the vestibular apparatus in the ears to transmit an orienting signal to the animal's neck muscles. The head is twisted into an upright and horizontal position and the rest of the body twists and lines itself up accordingly before landing.

SEXUAL BEHAVIOUR

Both male and female domestic cats reach sexual maturity when very young, little more than kittens in fact, and will readily reproduce unless confined or neutered. Females are able to produce two or three litters each year.

Female kittens may reach sexual maturity as early as five months old, and may then come into season every three weeks during the breeding season, even though they will not be physically fully grown until they are over one year old. Male kittens may reach sexual maturity from six to eight months old, although in some pedigree breeds this may be delayed for as long as 18 months. Domestic cats destined for life in the family home make much better pets when they are de-sexed, which removes their often unsocial sexual behaviour patterns.

Above *As they approach puberty kittens will often show the first signs of sexual gestures in their usual greeting and play behaviour.*

Below *Sexual differences.*

Male

A mature male cat is able to mate at any time, though he will be more sexually active in the spring and summer months. He is initially attracted to the female by the special evocative odour that she emits during oestrus, and also responds to her inviting cries. The scent and cry of the female cat in oestrus is said to carry over long distances, and any mature male cats in the vicinity will respond. When the cats meet, the rolling and posturing of the female further excites the male, who will mount and mate with her as quickly as possible. In a natural environment, several males may be attracted to one female and will bicker and fight for dominance and the privilege of mating. Sometimes a

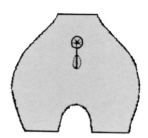

Female adult
The vulva is a vertical slit about 1cm (0.4in) from the circular anal opening.

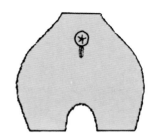

Female kitten
The vulva is a vertical slit almost joined to the circular anal opening.

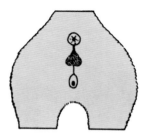

Male adult
The testicles are clearly visible in the male, set between two openings at least 2.5cm (1in) apart.

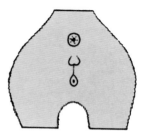

Male kitten
The tiny round opening in which the penis is concealed is about 1cm (0.4in) below the circular anal opening, with an indication of the scrotal sacs as slightly raised areas.

subordinate male will mate with the female while his superiors are engaged in battle. During her oestrus period, the female cat will mate many times, either with the same male, or with several different males.

Entire male cats which roam freely treat their homes as bases for food and shelter only. They are totally motivated by their strong sexual drive and spend their days patrolling their territories, marking their boundaries with spurts of pungent urine to deter interlopers. They constantly search for sexually receptive females to fight over and mate with, but often need to take time off for rest and recuperation. When male cats fight, their long, sharp, canine teeth inflict deep puncture wounds in their opponents, and the raking of their hooked claws causes deep scratches, all of which take a long time to heal. A cat fight between two males is bitter and serious. The cats confront each other, making huffing sounds, with cheeks puffed out, sometimes salivating and emitting low, fierce growls. They hunch up their shoulders and hips to look as large and powerful as possible. They circle, stiff-legged, then each cat lunges at the other's throat, biting hard.

The cats lock together in a rolling ball and rake each other with the back claws, causing lots of flying fur. When they break apart, one may run away and receive a final, deep bite at the root of the tail or the testes. On subsequent meetings with the vanquished cat, the dominant male may underline his superiority by biting the submissive male on the neck and mounting him briefly, before releasing him and walking away with stiff legs and tail. A male previously beaten into submission usually does his best to avoid any such confrontations, or will crouch down, offering the scruff of his neck to the dominant cat. Males rarely fight with females, but females will fight, particularly in defence of their kittens.

Female

Oestrus, or breeding condition, in the female cat is easy to recognize and consists of four stages. In pro-oestrus, the reproductive organs undergo changes in preparation for mating and pregnancy. The cat is extra affectionate, solicits stroking and restlessly roams around the house seeking a way out. After five days of the first stage, true oestrus begins, lasting for about seven days, during which time the cat will be ready and willing to mate. When stroked she assumes the mating position (see page 194). She may become agitated and roll on the floor as if in pain. Most cats wail, and in some pedigree breeds, such as the Siamese, the wailing can be indescribably loud and prolonged. If mating does not take place, the third stage, meto-oestrus, begins and the reproductive system relaxes until the fourth stage of anoestrus is reached. During anoestrus, the female cat's behaviour is contented and calm until the next cycle begins.

The queen, which s ready for the attentions of a boy friend, will quite often go crazy, crouching, rubbing and rolling. If stroked at this time, she will assume the mating posture (left). If a likely male happens to be in the vicinity, she will call to him (right) and tread with her legs. Courtship is the first of three stages in the mating process, and it usually takes from 10 seconds to five minutes.

THE FIRST DAYS

The newly-born kitten and the very elderly cat have two things in common. They are both relatively helpless. The kitten has the advantage of a doting mother to guide it into early adolescence. The older cat has the slight advantage of experience. They both have relatively large heads which tend to wobble. This is common to all newborn kittens and aged cats who die of nothing other than old age.

How can that short and skinny neck which contains seven cervical bones carry the weight? The first two bones are so modified that the cat can turn its head from side to side as easily as it can turn it up and down. And they are supported by muscles that any other species would envy. It seems miraculous that a mother cat can carry a kitten that weighs almost as much as she does over big fences and for considerable distances, but physiologically they are well-geared for that sort of task.

The newly-emerged kitten has limbs that are weak and uncoordinated, it flounders and paddles. As the kitten gradually becomes more sure-footed, its limbs begin to act like legs, but they are still relatively pliant. The logic of that evolutionary plasticity is simple.

The growing animal is prone to all sorts of accidents. Pliant bones don't fracture easily, and if they do, they heal very easily. The exceptions are those cats which are not allowed a natural diet which includes bones or bone meal.

During the middle stages of development – late kittenhood, adolescence and maturity – the cat's shape gradually changes according to geometric principles. The athletic youngster is roughly triangular, with a broad back which tapers into a very tiny abdomen. Later, the adult becomes rectangular. During late maturity and merging into old age, the muscles at the top tend to waste and the waist below becomes more prominent. The triangle has become inverted. This simple rule of thumb is an aid to telling the difference in ages between cats, and shows a cat that has prematurely aged through serious illness.

Right *The newly-emerged kitten is relatively helpless and it can only drag itself about.*

Newborn kitten

As it grows up it is much more sure-footed.

Kitten

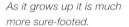

The body shape changes as it reaches adolescence. This youngster has a triangular shape, muscular shoulders with a smaller abdomen.

Adolescent

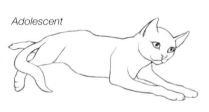

Later, the adult becomes much more rectangular.

Mature cat

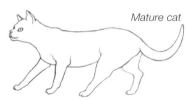

Old age brings a complete reversal as the triangle of youth is inverted, the muscles at the top tending to diminish and the waist becoming more prominent.

Elderly cat

The suckling kitten

The kitten at birth is deaf and blind, and almost completely helpless. It can move only a limited distance by using a sort of rock-and-roll shuffle accompanied by a characteristic head shaking.

However, it has an acute sense of feeling. The mother licks the kitten and by instinct it orientates itself from the mother's mouth towards the nursing area. The kitten crawling about in a haphazard manner usually has first contact with the outstretched legs of the mother while she is lying supine and follows the legs upwards until it finds a nipple.

The feeding behaviour of the newborn kitten has two instinctive elements. The first is the search for the nursing area and the second is the response to the nipple. During the first few days the response seems to be to the same teat. Later on the growing and ever more hungry kitten becomes less fussy.

There are three major phases in the relationship of the nursing kitten and its mother. During the first phase the mother initiates the whole feeding process. During the second, when the kittens are more independent, the relationship is more reciprocal. The kittens waddle towards the mother, and she assists the odd laggard. During the third phase, the kittens actively demand to be fed. They will follow the mother about until she stands or lies and allows them to feed.

Even at this last stage, the most callous of mothers will quickly respond to the pitiful call of a kitten which has wandered. She will not rest until she has found it and carried it to a place of safety.

Below *A nursing mother may reject one or more of her litter which appears to her to be sub-standard. This rejection is almost always irreversible. Nothing will persuade the mother to accept a once-rejected kitten. However, she may accept and rear a creature quite unlike herself, like a puppy. This behaviour, stimulated by hormones, is a physiological not a psychological reaction.*

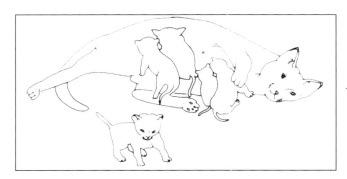

Below left *Many animals, including kittens, lick their mother's mouths; in this way, the mother passes on antibodies which help to fight disease. The habit also reinforces the links between the mother and her young.*

Centre and below *Sometimes kittens seem to burrow underneath the mother. The mother has two rows of nipples, and each kitten knows on which side it customarily feeds.*

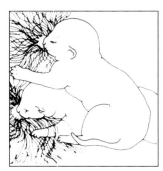
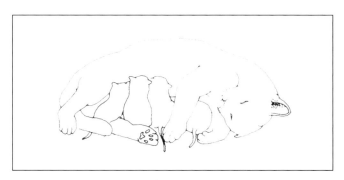

Learning Behaviour

No kitten can be expected to go from the coddled security of milk and nest directly into the skilled activity of hunting for food.

During kittenhood and adolescence, the young cat learns the skills that in maturity become second nature. The highest form of learning is *insight learning* which is the conscious consideration of a problem. In the laboratory it is difficult to devise experiments which simulate problems in the field, but it can be shown that higher animals, especially monkeys and apes, are capable of insight learning. Chimpanzees, for example, will pile boxes one on top of another so that they can reach a reward of fruit. Cats do not learn through insight; their instinctive behaviour is modified through experience, habituation and inhibited play.

It is difficult to distinguish between learned and instinctive behaviour. A litter of kittens may be left on their own for some hours while the mother goes off hunting. If they are left in a relatively cold nest they will instinctively cuddle together. The group can keep itself warm whereas a kitten on its own might rapidly lose body warmth and die. The same litter, left in a very warm area, will spread themselves out. This is almost certainly instinct.

A kitten learns through experience, or *trial and error*. This means that if a cat accidentally performs an action which is rewarded it may then deliberately do it again in the expectation that the reward too will be repeated. This is how many cats gradually learn the difference between the many possible expressions of their family of fellow cats, dogs and people. They will learn that every time they approach an individual who is not interested in play they receive a painful bite, scratch or kick. After a while, even the most energetic kitten learns that it is best to pause and take stock before rushing in. Similarly, a playful kitten, while jumping about, might accidentally open a cupboard door. It may learn to open the same cupboard door by imitating the mother. A whole world of forbidden titbits is revealed.

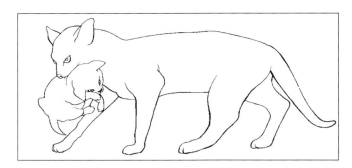

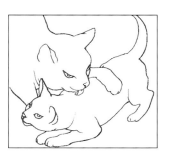

Above A cat may have chosen to rear her litter in the bedroom, despite the fact that she continues to be fed in the kitchen. No matter how clever the cat, she is simply not designed to carry a bowl of milk. The cat pictured above has solved the problem. She carries her litter to the bowl and they follow her example and lap the milk provided for them.

Left When the kittens are very young the mother can groom them at will. Just the action of her tongue is sufficient to control their playfulness. As the kittens grow she may have to use her powerful and flexible front paw to restrain them.

CATS COMMUNICATING

Besides producing identifiable sounds, cats also communicate in other non-vocal ways: body language, touch and scent. Cats' body language consists of a wide variety of postures and movements involving just about any part of the body, from the eyes and ears to the tail and the hair.

Ears pointed forwards convey friendly interest and attentiveness or suspense. Ears pricked and slightly back warn that attack is coming. Ears back and sideways signal defensiveness, fear and readiness to flee. Flattened ears suggest fear or submission. When hunting, ears are drawn back, contributing to a watchful appearance. A contented cat sits with its eyes half closed and ears upright.

Erect ears communicate annoyance, and eyes are likely to be narrowed to a vertical slit. Narrowed pupils are a sign of tension, heightened interest and aggressive threat, whereas dilated pupils express surprise, fear and defensiveness. Since the size of pupils also depends on incoming light, moods cannot be gauged by eyes alone.

In moods of excitement and fearfulness, cheek muscles pull the cheek ruff down towards the throat, sometimes in pulsing rhythm. Whiskers, if pointed forwards and fanned, indicate tension and attentiveness; if sideways and less fanned, calmness and comfort; if bunched and flattened, shyness.

Yawning expresses reassurance and contentment. Spitting is a sudden gesture used when frightened or angry, often accompanied by forepaws hitting the ground, arching of the back and raising of the fur along the spine. Although no attack usually occurs, cats achieve their purpose of threatening or warning just by using the bluffing gesture.

Below Perky ears and relaxed whiskers mark the face of a happy cat (1). An angered cat will push back its erect ears, narrow its pupils to slits, and push its whiskers forward (2). Flattened ears and whiskers and widened pupils show that a cat is frightened (3). A cat opens its pupils, perks up its ears and bristles its whiskers forwards when hunting and playing (4). A cat that is in ecstasy when being patted or when satisfied relaxes its eyes and whiskers (5).

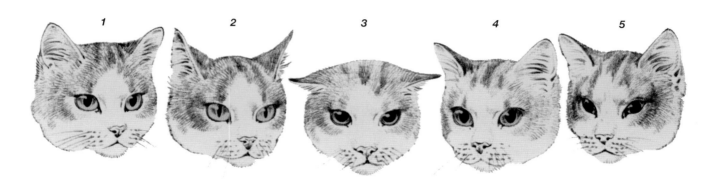

1   *2*   *3*   *4*   *5*

Above Cats may fight over territory, or a mate, but actual combat is always a last resort. More often, a ritual display of aggression is enough to see off an opponent. The combatants first investigate each other by sniffing at scent glands on the face (1). Swishing his tail, the aggressor sniffs the base of the opponent's tail and gives a threatening growl, putting the second cat on the defensive. The aggressor is now poised to strike (2) and the defensive cat crouches low, with ears and tail flat. The confrontation may end here, with the loser adopting a defensive posture and backing off (3). In this case the aggressor walks off disdainfully, leaving the loser to slink away. However, if the aggressor's challenge is met, fighting will ensue. The defendant first adopts the defensive threat, turning its body sideways and arching its back to look more imposing. The tail bristles and curls up (4). The aggressor, unimpressed, keeps on coming (5). The defendant crouches low, presses its ears flat to its head and hisses at its opponent. The pussyfooting is over (6). The aggressor pounces and the second cat defends itself by kicking out with its legs, claws out. The battle continues until the loser spots a chance to escape with as much dignity as it can muster.

The position of the head conveys messages, too. Stretched forwards, it means readiness for contact; if raised it means dominance; when lowered, inferiority; and when lowered jerkily with chin pulled in or turned sideways, it means lack of interest.

Legs stretched to full length show self-confidence or readiness for attack. Bent hind legs signify uncertainty or timidity; bent forelegs, desire to avoid conflict but willingness to defend if necessary; all legs bent, uncertainty, caution, or defensiveness.

A stretched-out body belongs to a confident or ready-to-attack cat. A constricted or arched back displays fear and defensiveness. When ready to mate, queens crouch in a position known as *lordosis*.

Quick, side-to-side tail movements indicate excitement. Rapid waving is an expression of annoyance. A still, raised tail is a friendly greeting and an invitation to sniff the anal region. An upright tail twitching slightly belongs to an alert cat. A tail that whips up suddenly is a threat of attack.

Mutual grooming reinforces the bond between two cats. When one seemingly clean cat does it alone, it may feel threatened or stressed. Cats also rub noses and rub against their owners and each other to signify acceptance and submission.

Left Chocolate Tortie. An entitre range of tortoiseshells gave rise with the introduction of the red or orange gene into Tonkinese breeding.

Below Lilac Smoke Persian. Both the Lilac Smoke and Chocolate Persians are accepted by several feline bodies and apart from colour, should conform to the basic standard of points.

BREEDS OF THE WORLD

Different breeds of cat have long inhabited many parts of the world. Throughout history migrations of the human population have been accompanied by migrations of the cat population. Since the mid-19th century there has been a great revival of interest in cats and cat breeding on both sides of the Atlantic and many new breeds have come out of North America and Europe. Here the breeds are listed according to country of origin.

On the following pages information is given on the origins of each breed, the physical attributes of the cats, their character and how to care for them. In the Key Facts boxes, diagrams show how each breed developed.

Naturally occurring

This symbol is used for a natural population which is now recognized as a breed.

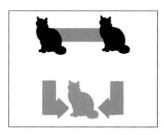

Cross breeding

This diagram shows how a man-made breed of cat has been developed by crossing two or more breeds.

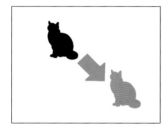

Mutation

This diagram shows how some breeds of cat come about because a mutation arises within a natural breed. This is due to an unpredictable change occurring in a gene. For example, the blue cat is a mutation of the black.

North America

Peke-Face Persian
Tortoiseshell-and-White
  Longhair
Colour point Longhair
Lilac Longhair
Chocolate Longhair
Balinese
Maine Coon
Somali
Cymric
Javanese
Ragdoll
American Shorthair
American Wirehair
Exotic Shorthair
Colourpoint Shorthair
Foreign Shorthair
Bombay
Tonkinese
Snowshoe
Sphynx
Malayan
Ocicat

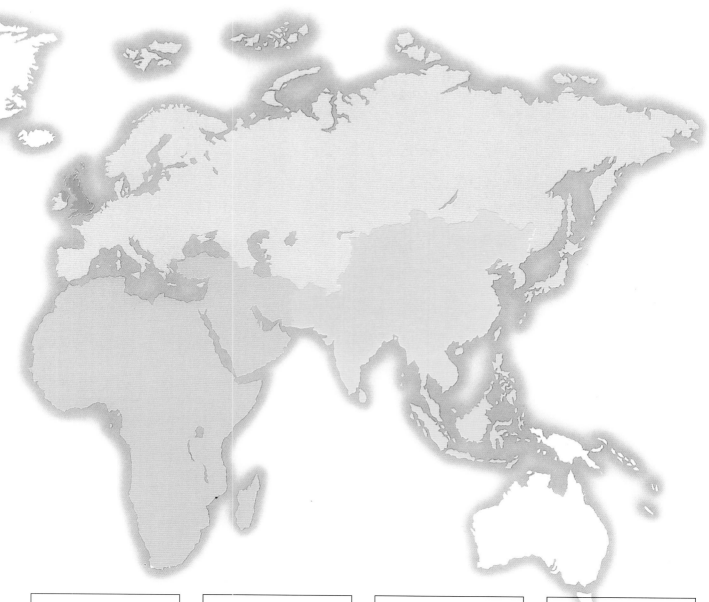

United Kingdom

Smoke Longhair
Chinchilla Longhair
Somali
British Shorthair
British Spotted Shorthair
British Bicolour Shorthair
Manx
Havana
Rex
Scottish Fold
Tiffany

Europe and Russia

White Longhair
Black Longhair
Cameo Longhair
Bicolour Longhair
Tortoiseshell Longhair
Norwegian Forest Cat
Russian Blue
European Shorthair

Middle East and Africa

Angora
Turkish Van
Abyssinian
Egyptian Mau

Asia

Birman
Siamese
Korat
Burmese
Japanese Bobtail
Singapura

ENCYCLOPAEDIA OF CAT BREEDS

LONGHAIR

WHITE LONGHAIR (WHITE PERSIAN)

Coat colour white.

Coat pattern/type various, thick fur with soft undercoat and longer guard hairs; plumed tail.

Eye colour various.

Build cobby with short thick legs round head with short nose and large eyes.

Character an able mouser, prefers indoor life, placid and not very active.

Care requires thorough daily grooming to prevent matting, varied diet with meat and multivitamins; kittens require constant attention.

Special problems over-feeding causing weight and heart problems; blue-eyed cats are prone to deafness.

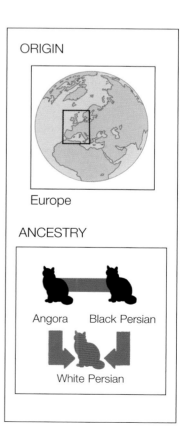

ORIGIN

Europe

ANCESTRY

Angora   Black Persian

White Persian

UNTIL THE 16TH CENTURY there were no longhaired cats in Europe. But a few cats of the type now known as Angoras were then introduced from Turkey, along with another, rather heavier longhair from Persia. The modern Persian cat, or Longhair as it is officially known in Britain (although many people still call it Persian and that remains its official name in America), is a descendant of those Persian cats. However, since the types were not always kept separate there was certainly some Angora blood mixed in during the early days of the Cat Fancy.

In Great Britain each colour type of the Longhair is considered an individual breed and, together with other longhaired breeds, they form one of the four groups into which cat breeds can be divided: Longhairs, Siamese, Shorthairs and Foreign Shorthairs. In the United States all the varieties are considered Persians of different colour types.

The White Longhair is a loving cat, quite affectionate towards its owners and those friends of its owners who treat it with respect and kindness. Generally calm, it is more tranquil and less active than many breeds. It is sociable towards other cats and rarely shows its claws. However, this cat can have a temper and can be demanding of affection. A skilled mouser, it also enjoys life inside and is well suited for living in a flat.

WHITE LONGHAIR (WHITE PERSIAN)

There are three varieties of White Longhair: orange-eyed, blue-eyed and odd-eyed. The odd-eyed, with one orange and one blue eye, is the result of interbreeding the other two varieties. Many blue-eyed white cats are born deaf.

The pure white coat of the White Longhair is thick and dense, yet silky. It forms a full frill – a lion-like mane – about the neck and shoulders. The body is of the solid, cobby type, broad but compact and powerful. Short, thick legs end in rounded, large paws. A bushy, short tail ends in a plume. A rounded, broad head features fully developed cheeks and a short nose. The eyes are round and large. The ears are rounded at the tip and relatively small.

Potential pedigree faults include too little hair, too thin a body, a difference in tail colouration, an elongated muzzle and ears that are too close together.

Intensive brushing with a soft-bristle brush is needed daily to prevent matting. The tail is a target for bothersome fleas and should be given particular attention. Dry shampoo should be used regularly.

Varieties *Orange-Eyed, Blue-Eyed and Odd-Eyed*

Longhairs thrive on a balanced but varied diet that daily includes meat with some cooked rice and vegetables. Multivitamin supplements are advised, particularly in the cat's first year. Overfeeding to the point of producing a fat cat can also cause heart problems.

During pregnancy and after delivery the female requires a great deal of care, including calcium and vitamin supplements to her normal diet. Likewise young kittens, until the age of four months, need constant attention.

BLACK LONGHAIR (BLACK PERSIAN)

Coat colour jet black.

Coat pattern/type silky and thick with full frill at neck and shoulders.

Eye colour dark orange or copper.

Build cobby with short thick legs, round head with short nose.

Character affectionate and prefers an indoor life, but is liveiy for a Persian and an able mouser.

Care requires thorough daily grooming to keep hair free from tangles, varied diet of meat, cooked rice and vegetables, plus multivitamins.

Special problems true black colouring is difficult to breed.

A TRUE BLACK LONGHAIR is a relatively rare animal. Many cats may seem black but on closer inspection actually have white or rust flecks in their coats. The glossy black colour is difficult to breed, and definitive results won't show in kittens until they are six or seven months old. The cat with the true black variation should be discouraged from basking in direct sunlight, which will bleach its coat, and dampness, which will cause a tint of brown. The Black Longhair is lively for a Longhair but retains the characteristic affection for its owners. Its jet black coat is silky and thick with a full frill at the neck and shoulders. The body is the cobby type. It has short, thick legs, rounded, large paws and a short, bushy tail, which ends in a plume. The head is rounded and broad with fully developed cheeks and a short nose. The eyes are round and large, either dark orange or copper in colour. Its ears are rounded at the tip and relatively small.

Common faults are hair not thick enough, a thin body, a tail of a different colour from that of the body, a too-long muzzle, and ears too close together.

To prevent matting, the fur needs daily brushing with a soft-bristle brush, with particular concentration on the tail, where fleas congregate. The diet should include meat, cooked rice and cooked vegetables. Multivitamin supplements are advised, particularly in the cat's first year.

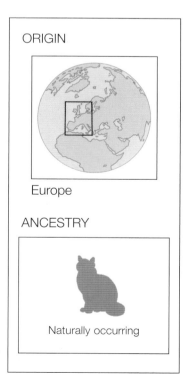

ORIGIN

Europe

ANCESTRY

Naturally occurring

RED LONGHAIR (PEKE-FACE PERSIAN)

Coat colour deep, rich red.

Coat pattern/type silky and thick with or without Tabby markings.

Eye colour dark orange or copper.

Build solid, cobby type with short thick legs, plume tail, round head with short nose.

Character calm, affectionate, sociable, prefers an indoor life.

Care requires thorough daily grooming to prevent matting.

Special problems possible respiratory and eating difficulties and overcrowding of the teeth, due to compression of facial features. Running eyes due to distortion of eye ducts.

ACTUALLY A VARIETY of the Red Persian – the only variety – the Peke-Face is bred to have a face resembling that of the Pekingese dog: a short nub of a nose, a clear dent between the eyes, wrinkles about the muzzle. This variety is quite rare, as the Red variety from which it springs is very rare itself.

The Peke-Face occurs naturally as a mutation of the Red or Red Tabby Persian, and it is encouraged in the United States. However, it is not encouraged in Great Britain because its compressed face is basically a deformity that can cause breathing, tear duct and eating problems.

Apart from the face, the Peke-Face carries most of the Persian traits. The ears are rounded, small and tufted. Its fur is thick and silky and of the Red or Red Tabby colouring. The body is of the solid, cobby type, with short, thick legs and round, large paws. The tail is short and bushy, ending in a plume.

Generally a calm cat, the Peke-Face Persian is affectionate towards its owners and others whom it has come to know as kind and gentle. It rarely shows its claws and gets along well with other cats, although it can have a bit of a temper. Life indoors is just fine for this cat. As with all Persians, the fur must be brushed daily with a soft-bristle brush to prevent matting.

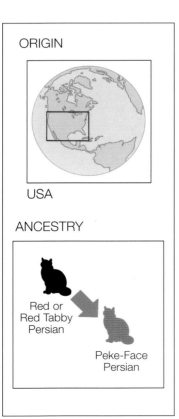

ORIGIN

USA

ANCESTRY

Red or Red Tabby Persian

Peke-Face Persian

CREAM LONGHAIR (CREAM PERSIAN)

IN THE EARLY DAYS, cream cats were often called 'fawns' and were often discarded by keen exhibitors in favour of cats with stronger coat colours. Some of the first Angoras were probably cream, for Charles H. Ross, writing in 1868, describes the Angora as '*a very beautiful variety, with silvery hair of fine silken texture, some are yellowish, and others olive, approaching the colour of a lion*'.

In 1903, Frances Simpson wrote that creams were becoming fashionable, but the first cats of this variety had been considered '*freaks or flukes*' and were given away. Cream cats were eventually imported into the United States from Britain and soon established themselves as successful show winners. Today's exhibition Cream Persian is a refined and sophisticated breed, exemplifying all the best features of the typical Longhair.

Coat colour pure and sound pale cream to medium colour.

Coat pattern/type fine, silky with or without shadings or markings.

Eye colour dark orange or copper.

Build solid, cobby type with short thick legs, plume tail, round head with short nose.

Character affectionate, sociable, prefers an indoor life.

Care requires thorough daily grooming to prevent matting.

Special problems will overeat if allowed to do so, tail can be a target for fleas.

ORIGIN

UK

ANCESTRY

Blue Persian   Red Persian

Cream Persian

SMOKE LONGHAIR (SMOKE PERSIAN)

Coat colour black, blue and tortoiseshell varieties.

Coat pattern/type long, dense and silky and thick with very long frill at neck and shoulders.

Eye colour orange.

Build cobby-type body with short thick legs, round and broad head with short nose, full cheeks.

Character quiet and home-loving but also a good mouser, affectionate and even-tempered.

Care daily grooming essential to prevent matting of fine fur. Varied diet with meat and multivitamins.

Special problems exhibition Smokes require special attention as wet weather and excessive sunlight will spoil appearance of coat.

THIS CAT FIRST appeared at shows in Great Britain in the 1870s, the result of cross breeding of Black, Blue and Chinchilla Persians. Although the coat appears to be of one solid colour, the effect is actually achieved by very long and very dark tipping. The pale undercoat is revealed only as the cat moves.

There are three varieties: Black Smoke Longhair, Blue Smoke Longhair, and Smoke Tortoiseshell Longhair (which is red, cream and black). Each variety has orange eyes.

The fur is silky, thick and dense, with a full frill that is white. The cobby-type body is stocky and broad, with short, thick legs and large, round paws. The short, bushy tail ends in a plume. The head is round and broad, the cheeks are full and the nose is short. The eyes are round and large. The ears are rounded, small, and tufted.

This cat is a good mouser but enjoys its home life as well. It demonstrates its affection for the family and friends and expects affection in return. Generally even-tempered, the Smoke Longhair accepts other cats into the household.

As with all Longhairs, the fur must be brushed daily with a soft-bristle brush to prevent matting of the fur.

Meat is a favoured diet item, balanced with cooked rice and vegetables. Multivitamin supplements are recommended, particularly during pregnancy and for kittens and growing cats.

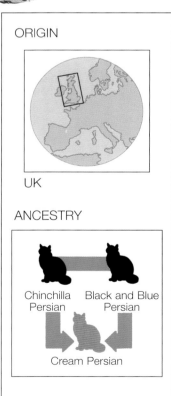

ORIGIN

UK

ANCESTRY

Chinchilla Persian   Black and Blue Persian

Cream Persian

BALINESE

WHEN BALINESE KITTENS first appeared as spontaneous mutations – the result of a recessive gene characteristic in some American Siamese bloodlines – they were referred to as Longhaired Siamese. But as a few breeders began to develop further the longhaired coat in their cats, a new name emerged. The name 'Balinese' was borrowed from the native dancers on the island of Bali, whose graceful movements inspired one of the breeders to rename this lithe and elegant cat. American organizations began to recognize the breed in 1963 and it was appearing in shows in Europe by 1970.

The Balinese can appear in all of the myriad colours of its ancestral Siamese line, but just four are recognized for championship status: chocolate, seal, blue and lilac.

Red, tortie and lynx point are generally considered as Javanese (see page 49). The eyes in all varieties should be blue. 'Slim and dainty' best describes this breed, which features the Siamese body lines with a heavier, longer coat. Its fur, however, is not as thick as most other longhaired breeds, and it lacks a ruff about the neck and shoulders. Its coat is extremely soft and silky to the touch, and it tends not to mat as much as other longhaired cats. The medium-length tail ends in a thick, fluffy plume.

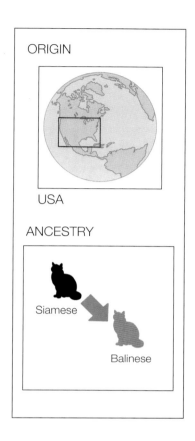

ORIGIN

USA

ANCESTRY

Siamese

Balinese

Coat colour chocolate, seal, blue or lilac points.

Coat pattern/type points on lighter background as Siamese; long fur, but shorter and silkier than other longhaired breeds.

Eye colour blue.

Build oriental, as Siamese, long, triangular head.

Character clever, lively and playful, generally quieter in demeanour and voice than some Siamese types, enjoys attention, suited to indoor life.

Care fur is less prone to matting, but daily grooming is appreciated.

Special problems reaches sexual maturity earlier than most longhaired cats.

HIMALAYAN (COLOURPOINT)

Coat colour seal, blue, chocolate, lilac, lame, tortie, blue-cream or lynx (tabby) point.

Coat pattern/type markings as Siamese, coat as Persian but tail less thickly furred.

Eye colour deep blue.

Build solid body, round head with plump features and extremely long whiskers.

Character intelligent, playful, gentle, devoted and very affectionate, seeks a lot of attention, skilled mouser, not aggressive to other cats, also well suited to indoor life.

Care requires regular brushing to keep coat free from tangles, varied diet with meat, cooked rice and vegetables.

Special problems crossed eyes, poor bone structure.

ORIGIN

USA

ANCESTRY

Siamese   Persian

Himalayan

TODAY'S HIMALAYAN features the unlikely combination of the Siamese pointed pattern on the long, flowing coat type of the Persian. This beautiful breed began in the mid-1920s, when a Swedish geneticist began crossing Siamese, Persian and Birman cats. His work was continued by geneticists at the Harvard Medical School through the mid-1930s, eventually producing the first Himalayan – named Debutante – in 1935. Although the scientists had named the first pointed longhair, they saw the work as nothing more than research without application for cat fanciers. With their results in hand, they were prepared to let the project drop.

But experimental breeding clubs, both in Great Britain and the United States, had learned of their work and had decided to continue development of the breed The British breeders, who thought Debutante was too close to Siamese to be a breed of its own, received a tremendous boost to their efforts in 1947 when a woman offered them the use of her queen. This cat was a longhaired Siamese of unknown pedigree but remarkably close to the standards of the Persian. That cat's genes proved crucial in the further development of the breed. The GCCF recognized the breed in 1955, calling it a Colourpoint.

The Himalayan name, however, was conferred by the American breeders, who borrowed the name from the Himalayan rabbit of the same colouration. The first Himalayans shown in the United States were unveiled in San Diego in 1957.

JAVANESE

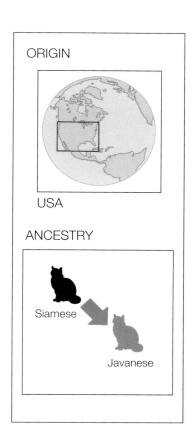

ORIGIN

USA

ANCESTRY

Siamese

Javanese

AS BREEDERS WORKED to develop the new Balinese breed, their crosses regularly produced a similar cat but of different colours from those they were trying for in the Balinese.

The name of another south-east Asian island – Java – was borrowed to describe what some saw as another new breed, the Javanese.

Different cat fanciers and organizations have chosen to view this cat in different ways: as a Colourpoint Shorthair with long hair, a Balinese in other Siamese colours, or a Siamese with long hair available in a great variety of colours. The varieties include: cream point, which is cream with pale yellow to reddish-yellow points; red point, cream with orangish-red points; tortie point, light brown to brownish orange with red and cream points; lilac-cream points, snow white with pink-grey and cream points; and lynx point, any of these colours in a tabby pattern.

Except for its colour, the Javanese is a Balinese cat. It has the same soft, mink-like coat, short by comparison to other longhaired breeds, and lacks an undercoat and ruff. Like the Balinese, it is a thin and delicate cat that displays the typical Siamese body lines but under a heavier, longer coat. It has the same medium-length, plume-like tail.

The Javanese has an active, fun-loving nature, and is dedicated and intelligent in whatever it chooses to do. It has the same gentle voice and demeanour as the Balinese, as well as an intense longing for attention from a few family members of its own choosing.

Coat colour cream, red, tortie, lilac-cream or lynx points.

Coat pattern/type points on lighter background, shorter coat than many longhaired breeds.

Eye colour blue.

Build oriental, as Siamese.

Character a skilled mouser, very active and acrobatic.

Care the long coat is relatively easy to groom due to the lack of thick undercoat.

BIRMAN

THE EXACT ORIGINS of the Birman breed are not known, but it is reasonable to assume that the feline has existed in much its present form in the south-east Asian republic of Burma for centuries. There it is known as the Sacred Cat of Burma and it occupies a special place in the religious lore of that country.

According to legend, the cats served as sentries in the Buddhist temples in ancient times. When invading hordes raided the temple of Lao-Tsun (a goddess of gold with eyes of blue gemstones) – they killed the head priest as he worshipped at the goddess's statue. The old priest's faithful cat, a pure white specimen, leapt onto the body of its dead master to protect it from further injury. Immediately, its white body was transformed to gold, like that of the goddess, except for its paws, which remained white. Its face, ears, tail and legs took on the colour of the Earth and its previously yellow eyes turned to sapphire blue.

For seven days, the cat remained, refusing all food and preventing anyone from touching the body. Finally it died and its soul escorted the soul of the priest into the afterlife. The other priests returned to select a new head priest. Their own white cats also returned, but now they all carried the markings of the dead cat.

The Birman is accepted in four colours, all having the characteristic white gloves: chocolate, which is gold-cream with warm chocolate points; seal, which is gold-cream with dark brown points; blue, which is gold-cream with blue-grey points; and lilac, which is white with pearl-grey points.

The Birman's medium-to-large body features large bones and a good musculature, with medium-length, strong legs, short paws and a bushy tail. Its head is broad and round and bears a strong muzzle, heavy whiskers, and almond-shaped eyes that are slightly slanted.

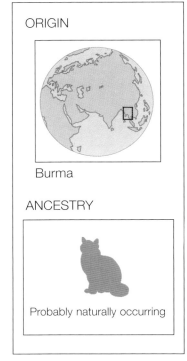

ORIGIN

Burma

ANCESTRY

Probably naturally occurring

Coat colour chocolate, seal, blue or lilac points.

Coat pattern/type white paws, bushy tail.

Eye colour blue.

Build large bones, strong legs, broad and round head, almond shaped eyes.

Character loving and faithful, gentle and even-tempered, but less placid than Persians, suited to indoor life but also enjoys some space outside.

Care regular brushing and combing will keep the long silky coat in good condition, prefers a diet of pure meat.

Special problems crossed or off-colour eyes, pointed muzzle, deformed tail.

CYMRIC

Coat colour various.

Coat pattern/type various, medium to long coat with heavy undercoat.

Eye colour various.

Build stocky, muscular body, long back legs, no tail and rounded rump, round head with strong chin.

Character lively, intelligent and affectionate, tolerant even of dogs, skilled mouser, enjoys outside exercise but is also home-loving.

Care coat not prone to matting but regular brushing appreciated.

Special problems prone to spina bifida; supplementing diet of breeding queens with vitamin B may help to reduce incidence.

CYMRIC (pronounced kim-rik) is the Celtic word for Welsh. In this instance, it refers to the Isle of Man, where the ancestral Manx breed began.

The Cymric is a longhaired Manx that was first discovered in an otherwise normal Manx litter in Canada in the mid-1960s. The first Cymric kittens arose from carefully pedigreed Manx lines that bore no record of Persian influence. Breeders determined that the long fur was the result of recessive genetic traits, and began mating the new cats Cymric to Cymric, producing litters that were fully Cymric. Too much crossing of the tailless cats, however, also brings out lethal genetic deformities, and so tailed or stumpy-tailed cats must continue to be crossed into the line.

Although only a few North American organizations accept the Cymric (for showing but without championship status), the breed's standards have been established to pinpoint the essential feature of the Cymric, which is its total lack of a tail.

The Cymric's coat is medium to long – although always shorter than that of the Persian – with a heavy undercoat. The outer hairs are lustrous and smooth. All colours and patterns are accepted in the breed at this point.

Like its Manx progenitors, the Cymric is an intelligent and playful cat, generally docile but an excellent hunter and climber. It is friendly towards the entire family and anyone else who visits its home. The breed seems to do best when living exclusively indoors.

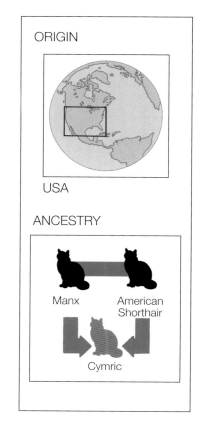

ORIGIN

USA

ANCESTRY

Manx   American Shorthair

Cymric

KASHMIR

Coat colour chocolate or lilac-cream.

Coat pattern/type solid colour, silky, dense fur.

Eye colour copper.

Build solid, with short, thick legs, short bushy tail with plume, round wide head and short nose.

Character loving and gentle, good hunter.

Care daily brushing to prevent matting, needs varied diet with meat, cooked rice and vegetables.

AS THE AMERICAN breeders were working to develop the chocolate-point and lilac-point Himalayans, solid chocolate and solid lilac kittens occasionally turned up in the litters. When these cats were bred to each other, the offspring shared the pure-coloured coats. Some organizations viewed these cats as a new breed, naming them Kashmirs, but others saw them as a division of the Persian or the Longhair. They continue to cause disagreement today.

The chocolate Kashmir is medium to dark brown with copper eyes. Apart from the solid colouring, all Himalayan characteristics have carried over into the Kashmir breed. The silky, dense fur covers a solid body with short legs, large round paws and a short bushy tail. The head is wide and round with round cheeks, a short nose, heavy whiskers and small ears with thick tufts.

Also like the Himalayan, the Kashmir is a well-behaved loving cat that is gentle towards humans and other cats but a great hunter of small prey. It enjoys some exercise space, but is content with a totally indoor existence. It also enjoys choosing and inventing its own activities.

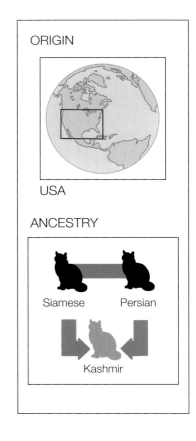

ORIGIN

USA

ANCESTRY

Siamese   Persian

Kashmir

LAVENDER KASHMIR (LILAC LONGHAIR)

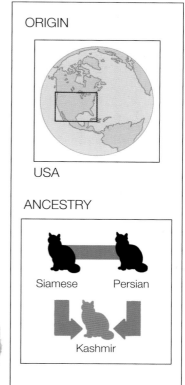

ORIGIN

USA

ANCESTRY

Siamese   Persian

Kashmir

AN OFFSHOOT OF selective breeding for Himalayans, the lilac colour of this cat's coat is a dilution which is linked to the Siamese so, although accepted as a colour variation of the Longhair in Britain, in the United States it is seen as a separate breed called Lavender Kashmir. It has the orange eyes and the thick, silky coat of its Persian ancestors but with a new, pink-grey tint.

As with Persians, the body is a solid, cobby type with short, thick legs and large, round paws. The tail is bushy and ends in a plume. The round head features fully developed cheeks and a short nose. Eyes are round and large. Ears are relatively small, rounded at their tips and well tufted.

Because of its Persian-type coat, the Lavender Kashmir requires daily brushing with a soft-bristle brush to prevent matting. It's a good mouser and enjoys some time outdoors, but it is equally happy with an indoor existence.

Coat colour pink-grey tint.

Coat pattern/type thick, silky coat.

Eye colour pale orange.

Build solid, with short, thick legs, short bushy tail with plume, round wide head and short nose.

Character curious and enterprising, likes to be active. Very affectionate and loyal.

Care daily brushing to prevent matting, needs varied diet with meat, cooked rice and vegetables.

TURKISH VAN

ORIGIN

Turkey

ANCESTRY

Naturally occurring

WHILE BRITISH organizations do not recognize the Turkish Angora, American organizations do not recognize the Turkish Van (also called the Turkish). The latter cat is a true-breeding variety of the Angora that arose in the wintery Lake Van region of Turkey. Given its heritage, the Turkish Van loves swimming and splashing about in the water – the opposite reaction of the Angora.

In winter the soft, silky coat of the Turkish Van is quite similar to that of the Persian, but it is mostly shed in the summer. The coat is yellowish white, with reddish brown at the ears and on the tail, which is ringed with darker red.

The Turkish Van is a long, muscular cat, but with a delicate bone structure. The head is wedge-shaped with a long nose, large rounded eyes and large tufted ears that show pink on their insides. A loving cat, it eagerly spreads its affection throughout the family but gives most to a few chosen individuals. It exists best as an indoor cat with access to a garden or terrace. Daily brushing and combing, similar to that of the Persian, are recommended.

Coat colour chalk white with reddish brown at the ears and on the tail.

Coat pattern/type soft, silky; sheds in summer.

Eye colour light amber.

Build long, muscular with delicate bone structure, wedge-shaped head with long nose, large eyes and ears.

Character gentle, affectionate, enjoys water and will actively choose to bathe, not very active, suited to indoor life.

Care hearty appetite, daily grooming recommended.

Special problems can be slightly nervous.

TURKISH VAN

Auburn Turkish

The markings of the Turkish Van cat are responsible for the 'Van' designation in other varieties which are mostly white, with small discrete areas of colour.

Cream Turkish

The Cream Turkish cat may have light amber or blue eyes and the odd-eyed variety is also accepted where there is one blue eye and the other of light amber.

MAINE COON

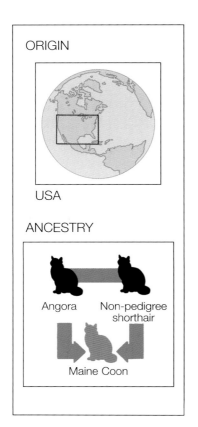

ORIGIN

USA

ANCESTRY

Angora   Non-pedigree
shorthair

Maine Coon

Coat colour any colour, except chocolate-point, lilac-point and Siamese.

Coat pattern/type extremely thick and shaggy, shorter near the head and front shoulders.

Eye colour copper, gold and green, with blue and odd-eyed also acceptable in the white Maine Coon.

Build large, great muscular definition, long bushy tail, with small plume, large paws, large, round head, tufted ears.

Character amiable and amusing, an ideal domestic pet, enjoys indoor life, but must have access to open space outdoors, an able mouser, tough, rugged and agile.

Care daily brushing to prevent matting, diet should alternate between meat and fish.

Special problems poor muscling and thin coat.

THIS DISTINCTIVE AMERICAN breed developed from American farm cat stock, which itself was the result of crossings of non-pedigree short-hairs and Angoras brought back to Maine by sailors. The Maine Coon was quite popular at US shows in the late 19th century, but interest declined with the introduction of Persians. It remained a welcome house pet, and in the 1950s exhibit interest began to resurface.

It is an excellent family cat, with its large, sturdy build, healthy constitution and intelligence. More than any other long-haired breed, the Maine Coon needs lots of open space. It enjoys the comforts of home, but it must have access to a garden and particularly likes a good, active romp in the outdoors. It needs to practise its mousing skills. Possibly because of its rough, outdoor, fend-for-yourself ancestry that led the breed to become accustomed to make-do sleeping arrangements, the Maine Coon will often be found asleep in unusual positions.

The Maine Coon is one of the healthiest cat breeds, able to endure wide ranges in temperature for prolonged periods – a hearkening back to its hardy ancestry. A litter holds two or three kittens, which very likely will bear little resemblance to one another. They develop slowly and won't reach full maturity until the age of four years.

MAINE COON

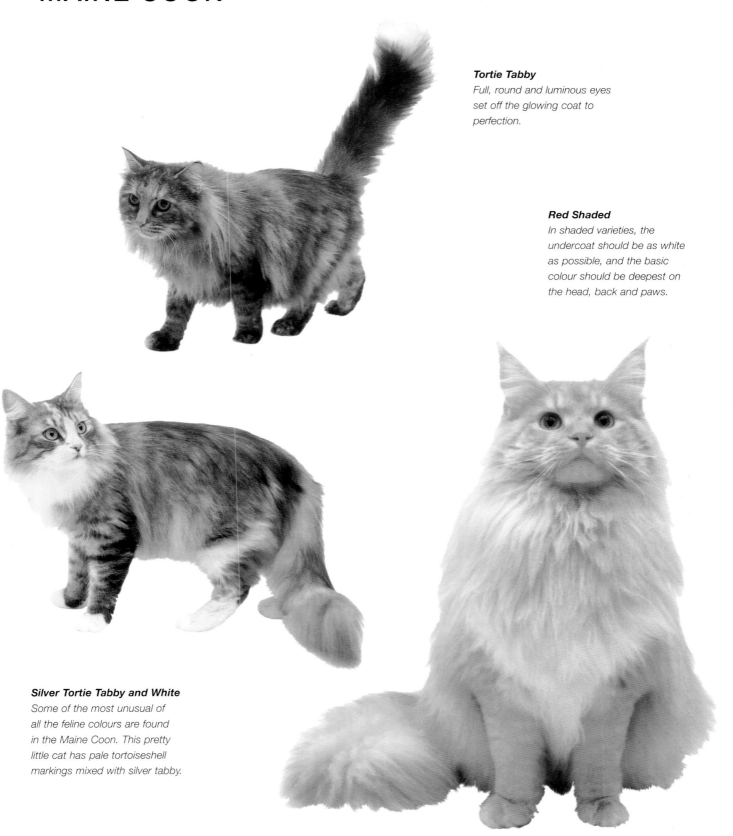

Tortie Tabby
Full, round and luminous eyes set off the glowing coat to perfection.

Red Shaded
In shaded varieties, the undercoat should be as white as possible, and the basic colour should be deepest on the head, back and paws.

Silver Tortie Tabby and White
Some of the most unusual of all the feline colours are found in the Maine Coon. This pretty little cat has pale tortoiseshell markings mixed with silver tabby.

TORTOISESHELL & WHITE LONGHAIR (PERSIAN)

Coat colour black, red and light red, or blue, cream and light cream white interspersed with white.

Coat pattern/type silky, thick and dense.

Eye colour deep orange or copper.

Build solid, cobby type, broad, compact and powerful.

Character placid, gentle, sociable and very affectionate, but demanding, skilled mouser, well suited to indoor and outdoor life.

Care daily grooming required to prevent matting, varied diet with meat and multivitamins.

Special problems tail is prone to flea infestation.

ORIGIN

UK and USA

ANCESTRY

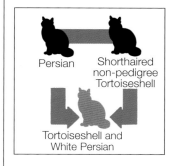

Persian   Shorthaired non-pedigree Tortoiseshell

Tortoiseshell and White Persian

THE TORTOISESHELL AND WHITE Longhair has the three tortoiseshell colours: black, red and cream (or their dilute forms with chocolate, blue or lilac replacing black), well distributed and broken and interspersed with white. In America some bodies recognize a similar cat but most call it the Calico Persian – because of a resemblance of the fur to a popular cotton print – and describe it as a white cat with black and red patching, much more white being apparent than in the British type and the underparts especially being white. Like the Tortoiseshell, this is a sex-linked variety and it appears in females only.

It's a loving cat, quite affectionate towards its owners and those friends of its owners who treat it with respect and kindness. Generally calm, the Tortoiseshell and White is more tranquil and less active than many breeds. It is sociable towards other cats and rarely shows its claws. However, this cat can have a temper and can be demanding of affection. A skilled mouser, it also enjoys life inside.

TURKISH ANGORA

Coat colour white, blue, black, blue smoke, silver tabby, red tabby, bicolour or calico.

Coat pattern/type medium-length, silky fur without undercoat.

Eye colour to suit coat colour.

Build fine bone structure; small, tufted paws; and a large, tapering but well-plumed tail.

Character gentle, peaceful and well-behaved cat, perfectly suited to an indoor life. It can remain motionless for incredible lengths of time.

Care easier coat than Persian, but still requires daily brushing and combing.

Special problems spotting on the body, short tail; blue eyed cats are often born deaf.

THE TURKISH ANGORA breed probably shares the same distant ancestors as the Persian, but the two breeds diverged when separate breeding populations became established in Turkey (Angora) and Persia (now Iran). The Angora was the first longhaired cat to be taken to Europe, first appearing in France and Italy in the 16th century. For a short time, British fanciers referred to it as the French cat because it was from that country that the breed entered England.

By the time of the first cat shows in the 19th century, however, the Persian was gaining preference over the Angora, which fell into rapid decline as a breed. As the 20th century dawned, only a handful of the Angoras remained in Turkey. Outside Turkey, the bloodlines had been severely diluted through crossings with Persians.

After World War II, the Angora enjoyed a small resurgence in popularity. Given the old name of the city of Ankara – Angora – the breed was recognized by the CFA in the early 1970s, but only white specimens were accepted until 1978. Today it is accepted in blue, black, blue smoke, black smoke, silver tabby, red tabby, bicolour and calico, although white remains the most popular colour. Several American breeders are currently at work with the breed, using cats imported from the Ankara Zoo in Turkey, where the breed is the subject of a major preservation effort as the Turkish national cat.

ORIGIN

Turkey

ANCESTRY

Naturally occurring

57

NORWEGIAN FOREST CAT

THE WILD AND FREE Norwegian Forest Cat evolved in the cold Norwegian forests, and was probably the result of crossings of shorthairs from southern Europe with longhairs from Asia Minor that were brought home by early Norwegian traders and explorers. Some bloodlines also include Persian, which found its way to Norway in the same manner, although the Norwegian Forest Cat is not a Persian hybrid.

It is also a breed of long-standing, described both in ancient Norse mythology and (as a 'fairy cat') in the region's fables dating as far back as 1837. It is held in high esteem in its native land as a living monument to Norwegian culture.

Reflecting its wild, outdoor past, the breed exhibits a thick double coat that provides extremely effective insulation against the cold northern winters. A shorter, woolly undercoat holds in body warmth, while a longer outer coat provides resistance to snow and rain. The cat sheds almost its entire coat each summer, retaining long hair only on the tail, paws and ear tufts. The coat should be combed, not brushed, and only occasionally.

The cat reveals its heritage further in its love of the outdoors and in its inventive ability to teach itself many tasks, such as opening latches to let itself into and out of the home. It also possesses some of the strongest claws among all domestic cats and is an excellent climber, even on rocky surfaces.

Breeders began actively working with the Norwegian Forest Cat in the 1930s, and again after World War II and in the 1970s. The Fédération Internationale Feline d'Europe recognized the breed in 1977, but it has yet to be recognized in the United States.

Coat colour all colours, except Siamese.
Coat pattern/type thick double coat with shorter undercoat.
Eye colour to suit coat.
Build medium to long body, stout legs, barrel chest, long, heavily furred tail that is carried high, rounded head, large round eyes, large tufted ears, strong muzzle.
Character hardy outdoor breed, good hunter, extremely agile climber, intelligent and independent, good natured and enjoys human company.
Care needs plenty of access to outdoors, varied diet of meat and fish, occasional combing.

ORIGIN

Norway

ANCESTRY

Naturally occurring

NORWEGIAN FOREST CAT

Red and White

Although the amounts of white are not specified for this breed, this cat does look even more attractive having neatly matching white paws and a small bib.

Brown Tabby

This handsome cat is marked with the classic tabby pattern which shows clearly on the smooth semi-longhaired cat.

RAGDOLL

THE RAGDOLL ORIGINATED in California and remains relatively rare outside the United States.

This is a controversial breed, which relaxes completely when picked up or held. The resulting floppy 'ragdoll' appearance gives the breed its name. The typical posture of the Ragdoll is flat on its side and completely relaxed.

Popular myth holds that the breed originated in the offspring of a female White Persian, injured when she was hit by a car. In this genetically unlikely scenario, those injuries led to a cat that cannot feel pain or face up to threats of any kind. The more scientifically based explanation for these unusual qualities in the Ragdoll is the heavily selective breeding that resulted in this cat. It does in fact have an extremely high tolerance to pain, to the point that injuries can go unnoticed. It also has an overly mild nature. Therefore, the Ragdoll is best off when living completely indoors, a situation it seems happy to accept. The ideal owner is someone who is able to satisfy the cat's need for tranquillity and some protection.

Varieties include the Bicolour Ragdoll, with a pale body, dark markings on the mask, ears and tail (seal, chocolate or lilac), and a white underside; Colourpoint Ragdoll, which has points in those same colours; and Mitted Ragdoll, which is the same as Colourpoint but with white front paws.

The fur is full and long, but not as long as many longhaired breeds.

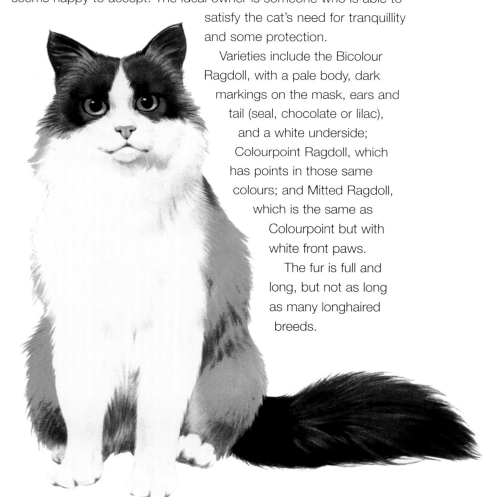

Coat colour seal-point, blue point, chocolate point and lilac point.

Coat pattern/type full, long and silky.

Eye colour blue.

Build long, solid body, medium legs, large paws, rounded wedge-shaped head.

Character has an extremely docile temperament, enjoys the quiet life indoors, goes limp when picked up.

Care daily combing with the hands or a soft brush will keep the coat in good order.

Special problems elongated muzzle, deformed tail and crossed eyes.

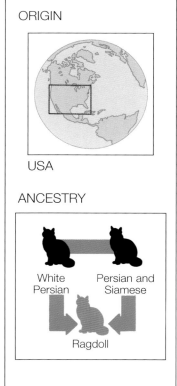

ORIGIN

USA

ANCESTRY

White Persian

Persian and Siamese

Ragdoll

SOMALI

Coat colour red and ruddy, silver, blue and lilac also produced.

Coat pattern/type medium long, ticked fur with darker bands.

Eye colour gold or green.

Build long, slender body and tail, fine boned legs, small paws, rounded wedge-shaped head, large ears and almond-shaped eyes.

Character shy, cautious and affectionate, intelligent, athletic, enjoys access to outdoors, dislikes confined spaces.

Care regular brushing will prevent matting, diet should include meat and giblets.

Special problems will overeat if allowed to, cannot tolerate cold, requires special care during winter.

ORIGIN

USA

ANCESTRY

Abyssinian

Somali

THE SOMALI is a pleasantly wild-looking off-shoot of the Abyssinian that first appeared in litters of otherwise normal Abyssinians in the United States in the mid-1960s. The resulting kittens were longhaired Abyssinians, at first thought to be simple outcrosses to a longhaired breed. But research revealed that some bloodlines of the Abyssinian had indeed carried the recessive gene for long hair through several generations. With inbreeding that recessive gene was able to manifest itself in some lines, as long as the recessive longhaired gene was present in both parents.

The CFA granted championship status to the new breed in 1978, one year after it was officially presented at shows in Europe. Its first showings had come much earlier, in 1965, in Australia. Those organizations that do recognize the breed follow the same standard as that employed for the Abyssinian breed but with medium-to-long fur that is slightly ticked, a noticeable ruff, more heavily tufted ears and a bushy tail. Only red (red tipped with brown) and ruddy (orange-brown tipped with black) varieties are currently accepted, but breeders have been producing silver, blue and lilac for several years.

Although the Somali should be allowed outside during warmer months, the cat must be sheltered from winter weather. It is a skilled hunter, and a glutton for meat and giblets. Sometimes mistrustful in new situations, the breed enjoys the company of those humans and other cats that it has come to know.

The Somali female gives a litter of only two or three very small kittens. They are very dark at first, and the distinctive ticking comes on to the coats only with maturity at about 18 months.

BICOLOUR LONGHAIR (BICOLOUR PERSIAN)

Coat colour any solid colour with white.

Coat pattern/type thick hair with soft undercoat, clear and even patching.

Eye colour light amber.

Build cobby with short, thick legs, plumed tail.

Character placid, of gentle temperament, not very active, good mouser, breeds well.

Care long coat requires regular grooming.

Special problems uneven colour patches, elongated muzzle, ears too close together, coat too thin.

WHEN THESE CATS first appeared at shows, they were placed in the 'any other colour' class. But eventually, as they demonstrated their staying power, they were given a class of their own. The original standards mandated an exact symmetry in their patching, but today any even patching is acceptable.

A beautifully contrasting cat, the Bicolour Longhair features solid colours with white muzzle, chest, undersides, legs and feet. A white frill also is now permitted and any recognized solid colour with white is an acceptable Bicolour Longhair variety. The eye colour should complement the solid colour.

It's an affectionate cat, good-natured towards other creatures that treat it kindly and gently. Not an overly energetic cat, it is nonetheless a good mouser. It's perfectly content with life in a flat, although periods outside are appreciated.

In typical Longhair fashion, the coat is thick and dense, yet silky with the lionlike frill about the neck and shoulders. The body is solid, broad and powerful. The short, thick legs have rounded, large paws. A bushy, short tail ends in a plume. The rounded, broad head features fully developed cheeks, a short nose, round and large eyes and relatively small ears that are rounded at the tip and tufted.

Potential pedigree faults include uneven colour patches, too little hair, too thin a body, a difference in tail colouration, an elongated muzzle and ears that are too close together.

Intensive brushing with a soft-bristle brush is needed daily to prevent matting of the fur.

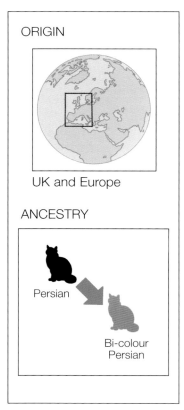

ORIGIN

UK and Europe

ANCESTRY

Persian

Bi-colour Persian

BICOLOUR LONGHAIR (BICOLOUR PERSIAN)

Cream and White Bicolour
*In the Bicolour the face is
required to show both coloured
and white areas.*

Black and White Bi-colour
*This massive cat has very good
markings, particularly the
desired white 'collar'.*

TIFFANY

Coat colour sable.

Coat pattern/type solid colour with lighter ruff long, silky fur.

Eye colour golden.

Build medium-sized with long body, rounded head with wide-set ears.

Character friendly, self-confident, humourous, likes attention, adaptable to both indoor and outdoor life, long lived.

Care daily grooming to prevent matting.

THE TIFFANY, actually a longhaired Burmese, was first produced in England in efforts to develop a solid chocolate Himalayan, which is now called a Kashmir. When Himalayans and Burmese were crossed, the litters contained several of the new longhaired breed.

The Tiffany, available only in sable with golden eyes, has the Burmese seal-brown coat but with a lighter, shimmering ruff. The coat is of medium length and quite smooth over the typical Burmese body. The face is somewhat fox-like with rounded eyes.

No organizations have yet recognized the Tiffany, which remains a relatively rare breed kept in existence by a handful of faithful breeders. It is a difficult breed to perpetuate because of the recessive longhaired gene involved; fewer longhaired kittens are born into each subsequent litter.

The Tiffany is a very playful cat, as long as the play is not too excited or strenuous. It is gentle, too, with a chirping, birdlike voice to match. Familiar creatures that share its home are generally the object of very vocal affection.

ORIGIN

ENGLAND

ANCESTRY

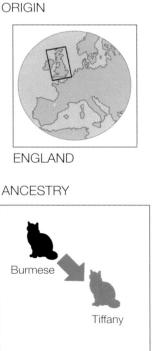

Burmese

Tiffany

TORTOISESHELL LONGHAIR (PERSIAN)

THIS VERY rare Persian is difficult to breed and consequently carries a higher price tag than most of the others. The genetic make-up necessary to produce the Tortoiseshell Persian also guarantees that the resulting cat is always female.

The cat was produced through the accidental crossing of Persians with non-pedigree, and probably shorthaired, tortoiseshell cats. Those individuals with a red or cream facial blaze from nose to forehead are much sought after.

Apart from its wild-looking coat, the Tortoiseshell Longhair is a typical 'Persian'. Affectionate and good-natured towards most other creatures that treat it kindly and gently, the cat forms attachments to the family as well as frequent-visiting friends. Life indoors is acceptable to this calm cat that enjoys the comforts of home.

The coat is silky, thick and dense. The customary Persian frill about the neck and shoulders might appear a bit 'wilder' in this cat than in other Longhairs. The body is solid, broad and powerful.

Short, thick legs end in rounded, large paws. A bushy, short tail ends in a plume.

The rounded, broad head can have a false heart-shape appearance in those individual cats with facial blazes. Otherwise, the features are full cheeks, a short nose, round and large eyes and relatively small ears that are rounded at the tip and tufted.

Intensive brushing with a soft-bristle bush is needed daily to prevent matting of the fur. Particular attention must be paid to the tail, where fleas can gather.

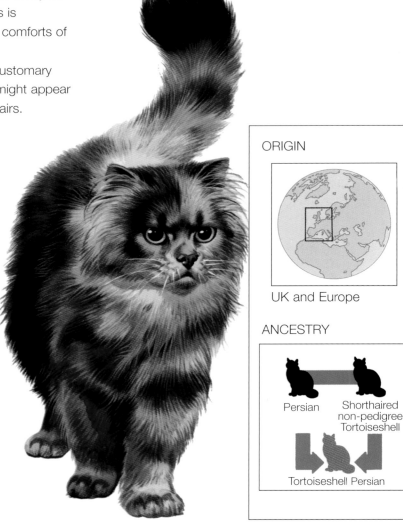

Coat colour black with unbrindled patches of red and light red, blaze of red and light red on face is desirable.

Coat pattern/type thick fur with soft undercoat and longer guard hairs.

Eye colour brilliant copper.

Build stocky, large bones, round head and eyes.

Character lively and intelligent home-loving and affectionate.

Care daily grooming required to prevent matting, varied diet with meat and multivitamins.

Special problems tail is prone to flea infestation.

ORIGIN

UK and Europe

ANCESTRY

Persian   Shorthaired non-pedigree Tortoiseshell

Tortoiseshell Persian

SHORTHAIR

ABYSSINIAN

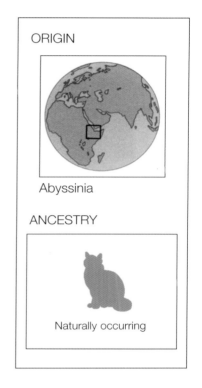

ORIGIN

Abyssinia

ANCESTRY

Naturally occurring

Coat colour agouti, red, blue, cream.

Coat pattern/type ticked hairs.

Eye colour gold to green to hazel.

Build medium, between Oriental and cobby with a modified Oriental head.

Character gentle, affectionate, quiet voice, highly active, intelligent, can be taught tricks, agile and likes plenty of space, indoors or out.

Care play and exercise are a vital part of daily routine, supplement diet with vitamins, groom daily with gloved hand.

Special problems pregnant females need special care as they remain quite active during pregnancy and falls can be common.

THE MUMMIFIED remains of some Ancient Egyptian cats are almost perfect copies of cats found in Abyssinia (today's Ethiopia) at the end of the 19th century. The Egyptian cats had 'ticked' (agouti) tawny hair, golden at the roots, and a similar-shaped head. There were also black and blue cats in Ancient Egypt. This led experts to believe that the Abyssinian (affectionately known as the 'Aby') and the Egyptian cat may have come from the same wild ancestor, the African Kaffir cat.

Others assert that the breed was established from tabby matings, a possibility because every now and then Abyssinian-type kittens are born to ordinary tabby

ABYSSINIAN

Usual Abyssinian
The rich golden brown coat ticked with bands of black gives this usual Abyssinian its unusual appearance. It is known as the Ruddy Abyssinian in Europe and America.

Abyssinians come in a number of different colours. Agouti and red are the most common, but there are also blue and beige or cream varieties. Their eyes range from gold to green to hazel. In both Britain and the United States, the ideal 'Aby' is a medium-sized cat of modified oriental type, with a firm, muscular body. American standard calls for a slightly rounder head. Faults include signs of cobbiness, white marks on the neck, and random spots on the legs, neck and tail.

The 'Aby' came close to extinction during both World War I and World War II, when food scarcities struck everywhere in Europe. Meat, which is an essential need for all cats, but more so for the Abyssinian, was in extremely short supply. It had recovered, however, by the 1960s and '70s, only to suffer a severe setback with the outbreak of the feline leukaemia virus.

Although it is rather rare, partly because it tends to bear small litters, the Abyssinian is a very popular cat, and is now enjoying another strong period of recovery.

Abyssinians are inquisitive animals and learn tricks quickly. They do, however cherish their freedom and will become quite restless if confined indoors. They are excellent climbers and, as with any display of their abilities, expect to be praised for it. Even when indoors they are happiest involved in some activity. Above all breeds, the Abyssinians need play with their owners as part of their daily routine. If play is neglected they will become sullen and isolate themselves even to the extent of abandoning their home.

parents. Even pedigree Abyssinians sometimes have kittens with tabby markings.

A male cat called Zulu, taken to Great Britain by soldiers returning from the Abyssinian War in 1868, became the basis for the British breeding programme. The breed was recognized in 1882 in Britain and by 1905 in the United States. These cats were initially known by other names besides Abyssinian, including Hare Cat, Rabbit Cat and Bunny Cat, because their coat is similar to that of the wild hare or rabbit. The coat is short, but has several bands of ticking.

AMERICAN SHORTHAIR

Coat colour various (see list over).

Coat pattern/type short thick and even, hard in texture, somewhat heavier in winter.

Eye colour various.

Build medium to large, powerful, well-rounded head, high cheekbones and round eyes.

Character ideal family pet, skilled hunter, hardy and resistant to cold, enjoys outdoors, affectionate and even-tempered.

Care easy to groom, no special dietary requirements.

Special problems long or fluffy coat, deep breaks in nose profile.

ORIGIN

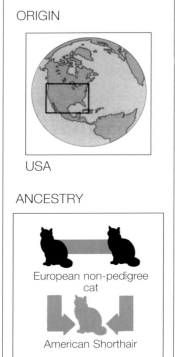

USA

ANCESTRY

European non-pedigree cat

American Shorthair

LIKE ITS BRITISH cousin and partial ancestor, the American Shorthair is very much a cat of the streets, the barnyards and the countryside. It was brought to North America on the same ships that brought the European settlers, to protect the ship's stores from mice and rats. Once ashore they interbred and adapted to a new lifestyle and environment.

The first officially recognized individual of the breed was Buster Brown, a cross between British Shorthairs and the emerging American cats; that was in 1904. As happened with the British Shorthair, breeders quickly began to breed from the best of the naturally occurring cats.

AMERICAN SHORTHAIR

Another characteristic the American Shorthair shares with its British counterpart is its hardy, healthy nature. Even larger and more muscular than the British Shorthair, this American cat epitomizes the pioneer spirit of the nation. It is a bold, inquisitive cat with a 'working' past that needs outside spaces to roam. Always ready to do something, the American Shorthair is happiest when active.

The breed will show affection to the entire family and friends, as long as it receives respect in return. It also demands praise when returning from a successful hunt with dead prey in tow.

Befitting a cat that originated in the outdoors, the fur is thick and dense, the body is athletic and strong, the legs are medium and powerful with large, round paws. The head is egg-shaped (with the more pointed ends on the sides of the head) with large, round eyes and a well-developed muzzle. The ears are medium in size, rounded at the tips, and lightly tufted.

American Blue Tabby
This classic tabby with its full-cheeked face is showing a good example of the 'M' on the forehead, formed by the clearly marked frown lines.

Coat colours

White	white coat, no markings, blue, gold or odd eyes.
Black	black coat, no markings, and gold eyes.
Blue	blue-grey coat, no markings, and gold eyes.
Red	red-brown coat, no markings, and gold eyes.
Cream	buff coat, no markings, and gold eyes.
Bicolour	white coat with blue, black, red or cream patches, gold eyes.
Shaded Silver	white undercoat, grey-tipped markings, green eyes.
Brown Tabby	brown coat with black Classic or Mackerel pattern, gold eyes.
Red Tabby	red coat with darker red Classic or Mackerel pattern, gold eyes.
Silver Tabby	grey coat with black Classic or Mackerel pattern, green eyes.
Blue Tabby	bluish coat with dark grey Classic or Mackerel pattern, gold eyes.
Cream Tabby	cream coat with darker cream Classic or Mackerel pattern, gold eyes.
Cameo Tabby	white coat with red Classic or Mackerel pattern, gold eyes.
Patched Tabby	silver, brown or blue coat, black or light silver Classic or Mackerel pattern, red or cream patches, gold eyes.
Chinchilla	white undercoat, black tipping, green, blue-green eyes.
Shell Cameo	white undercoat, red tipping, gold eyes.
Shaded Cameo	white undercoat, longer red tips than the Shell Cameo, gold eyes.
Cameo Smoke	white undercoat, red tipping, gold eyes.
Blue Smoke	white undercoat, blue tipping, gold eyes.
Black Smoke	white undercoat, black tipping, gold eyes.
Blue-Cream	bluish coat, cream patches, gold eyes.
Tortoiseshell	black with cream/red patches, gold eyes.
Tortoiseshell Smoke	white undercoat, black, red, cream tipping in tortoiseshell pattern, gold eyes.
Calico	white, red/black patches, gold eyes.

AMERICAN WIREHAIR

Coat colour various.

Coat pattern/type various; coat must be thick, springy and tightly curled.

Eye colour various.

Build medium to large, well-rounded, round head; high cheekbones and round eyes.

Character alert, inquisitive, independent, enjoys the comfort of home as well as the outdoors, affectionate and loving.

Care easy to groom, no special dietary requirements.

Special problems long or fluffy coat, deformed tail, deep breaks in nose profile.

THE AMERICAN WIREHAIR is a good example of spontaneous mutation. It happened in 1966 in Verona, New York State, to Adam, a red and white American Shorthair. Instead of the usual American Shorthair coat, he was born with a curly, wiry coat that bore more resemblance to a lamb's fleece.

Adam was taken by a breeder and mated with one of his littermates, a brown tabby tortoiseshell (torbie). Of their four kittens, two were red and white wirehairs. One of them, Amy, later gave birth to other wirehaired kittens. Among them was Barberry Ellen, the first true-breeding American Wirehair.

Both Adam and Amy were too long and slim for the American Shorthair standard, so breeders attempted to improve the body while retaining and thickening the wiry coat. Because the wirehaired gene is dominant, it was possible to outcross for these improvements without losing the coat trait.

The use of longhaired breeds for mating was avoided to maintain the distinct coat appearance. The ideal coat must not be patchy, although on underparts it should be less wiry. It should be of medium length, tightly curled, thick, coarse, resilient and springy. Faults are long or soft coat, and colours that might induce hybridization.

American Wirehairs have been bred in a variety of colours, and in 1977 were given championship status by the CFA. The name American Wirehair comes from the canine Wirehaired Terrier because the coats are so similar.

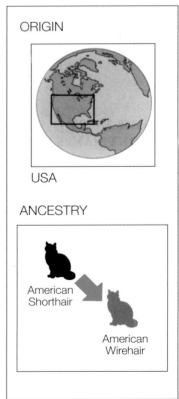

ORIGIN

USA

ANCESTRY

American Shorthair

American Wirehair

JAPANESE BOBTAIL

Coat colour any, except Siamese or Abyssinian agouti.

Coat pattern/type silky, medium-length fur.

Eye colour to match coat.

Build medium body, lean, hind legs longer than front legs, but angled so that their spines are level when standing, triangular head, high cheekbones, slanted eyes, large ears.

Character affectionate, ideal family pet, intelligent, needs lots of attention and play, well suited to indoor life.

Care light daily brushing, include plenty of fish in diet.

Special problems long or straight tails, kittens are large at birth, especially their heads and feet.

JAPANESE BOBTAIL CATS are regarded as lucky, and artistic representations of these Mi-ke (pronounced mee-kay, meaning three-furred) cats, with right paw raised, are symbols of good fortune.

The coat is a combination of red, black and white fur. The breed's other unusual feature is the short, multi-kinked tail held close to the body. The bobbed tail is about 10cm (4in) long and has thicker fur than the body, giving a pompom look. The tail's natural appearance is slightly deceptive, though, because when allowed to curl it looks much shorter than it actually is. Because of its similarity to a rabbit's tail, it is known as a Bobtail.

Although usually the silky, medium-length coat is red, white and black, a variety of colours is acceptable, except the Siamese or Abyssinian agouti patterns.

This cat was around long before it was first mentioned a thousand years ago in a manuscript written by a tutor to the Empress of Japan. Originally from China and Korea, it was a familar figure in prints and paintings, and is shown on the front of the Gotokuji Temple in Tokyo. It is said that the first cats to arrive in Japan were black, followed by white and then orange – thus the three-coloured fur came to be.

An American living in Japan sent the first three Bobtails to the United States after World War II. Later, when she returned, she took 38 cats with her. Japanese interest in the breed grew only after American judges visiting a Japanese show in 1963 praised them. They were recognized by the CFA in 1978, but the breed is still rare in the United States, and is not yet recognized in Europe.

Although similar to the Manx, Japanese Bobtails are not related to it. The Bobtail's tail is due to a recessive gene and breeds true. The Manx's tail, however, is a genetic defect.

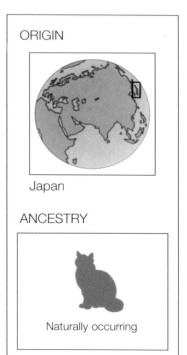

ORIGIN

Japan

ANCESTRY

Naturally occurring

KORAT

Coat colour blue with silver sheen.

Coat pattern/type short, thick and silky, no undercoat.

Eye colour green or amber-green.

Build stocky, muscular, medium-length tail, heart-shaped head, large eyes.

Character quiet, affectionate, makes an intelligent, loving pet. Playful, inquisitive, likes to perform tricks, prefers indoor life and is easily upset by loud noises.

Care groom by rubbing daily with a gloved hand; vaccination against viral infections is vital.

Special problems not a hardy breed, prone to chills and respiratory infections in cooler climates.

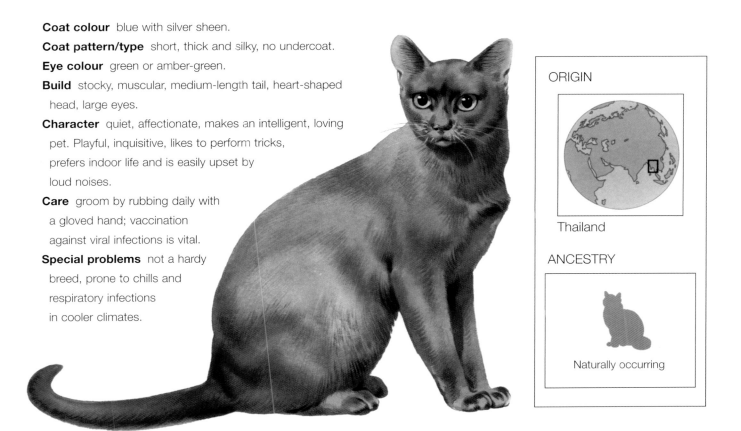

ORIGIN

Thailand

ANCESTRY

Naturally occurring

THE KORAT Is not a common breed. It is rare even in its native land of Thailand. Its an ancient breed with a long history. Originating in the province of Korat (*Si Sawat* in the local language), the cat was given the same name as the land. The name loosely translates into 'good fortune', and a pair of the cats was always among the traditional wedding gifts to Thai brides. The cats were also given to nobility as testimony of their subjects' loyalty and reverence toward them.

The Korat's affectionate, quiet nature is befitting of such an animal. The breed is also inquisitive by nature, knowledgeable about everything in its environment. The Korat prefers to be totally indoors; street noises and even a busy household are extremely upsetting to the animal. However, it remains playful with its human owners throughout its life. It is one of the very few breeds that seems to delight in learning and performing repetitive tricks on command. On the other hand, it is severely combative toward any strange cats brought into the home.

The first Korats were brought into the United States in 1959. Official recognition came in 1966, and the breed entered Great Britain in 1972. There are no varieties of the Korat beyond the solid silver-blue.

The fur is short, thick and silky, with no undercoat. The body is stocky and muscular, with a medium-length tail that ends in a point. The legs are medium and strong, ending in small, egg-shaped paws. The head has a definite heart shape to it, with a short nose but overall pronounced muzzle. Eyes are large, round, prominent and green or amber-green. Ears are very large and rounded at the points.

Both sexes make very devoted, playful and loving parents. Kittens do not reach their full potential colouring until about two years of age.

EGYPTIAN MAU

Coat colour bronze, silver, smoke.

Coat pattern/type spotted markings, barring on legs.

Eye colour light green.

Build between Oriental and cobby, with a slightly rounded head with large ears.

Character lively and affectionate, can be aloof with strangers, has a melodious voice, able mouser, well suited to life indoors.

Care requires protection from cold temperatures; feed on meat and giblets; gentle stroking with gloved hand will maintain coat.

Special problems no spots, wrong colour eyes.

ONE OF THE MORE prominently patterned breeds, the Egyptian Mau can have a spotted coat reminiscent of the leopard or a lined coat similar to that of the tiger. As might be expected, these imprints are very critical under the CFA standard. The forehead should display the classic 'M' pattern, with frown marks extending back and into spots on the spine.

Two 'mascara' lines around each of the eyes extend to the sides of the face. There is barring on the legs, with distinct matching spots being preferred on the body itself. On the underparts, spotting should contrast against the lighter coat colour.

Three body colours are permitted, and all are shown in the same class. The Bronze has a bronze background with a creamy underside and brown patterning. The Silver has a similar distribution of colour, set against charcoal-black markings. In the case of the Smoke, the charcoal body has black patterning.

The fur is dense but finely textured. The body is medium length and muscular, with medium legs and small egg-shaped paws. The head is triangular with a short nose, large, light green, almond-shaped eyes and large, slightly pointed ears.

All colours have brown or black paw pads, the Smoke has a black nose, while both Silver and Bronze have brick-red nose leathers.

ORIGIN

Egypt

ANCESTRY

Naturally occurring

EGYPTIAN MAU

A natural breed, the Egyptian Mau originates from Cairo where it is said to be descended from the cats which were worshipped in Ancient Egypt. Another theory is that it was just bred to look like that ancient cat.

In the 1950s, Princess Troubetskoye obtained a pair of Maus named Gepa and Ludol, which had originated in Egypt. It was not until some years later, in 1968 by the Cat Fanciers' Federation (CFF) and in 1977 by the CFA, that Americans finally gave recognition to the breed.

This type of cat resembles the Abyssinian. It is a blend between the oriental of the Siamese and the cobby of the longhair. They are active, muscular cats, of medium size with long legs. The head is slightly rounded with large, moderately pointed ears.

Both sexes are good parents, taking the best care of the kittens and spending great amounts of time playing with them.

Although they can be affectionate, they do not take naturally to strangers. Faults include blended or no spots, a small head, pointed muzzle, too-slanted eyes and the wrong eye colour.

The Egyptian Mau was imported to Britain for the first time in 1978. Prior to that, its description was used for another breed, now called the Oriental Spotted Tabby. There is a clear difference in body type between these two breeds. The Spotted Tabby has a more foreign appearance, probably from Siamese crossings. Its head markings are more pronounced, and it boasts a wider range of colours: blue, chocolate and lilac (where the eyes should be green); and red and cream (where eye colour can range from copper to vivid green).

Silver Mau

The Silver Egyptian Mau has clear markings in dark charcoal on a pale silver ground colour. The gooseberry green eyes complete the rather exotic effect.

CORNISH REX

Coat colour all colours.

Coat pattern/type short plush coat without guard hairs, curls, waves or ripples all over the body, crinkled whiskers and eyebrows.

Eye colour to match coat.

Build medium-sized, slender with wedge-shaped head and rounded muzzle, oval eyes, long tail.

Character intelligent, affectionate and rather extrovert by nature, playful and mischievous, makes a wonderful pet.

Care the unique curled coat does not shed hair, making it extremely easy to groom with hand stroking and the occasional use of a comb.

Special problems shaggy coat or bare patches.

IN 1950 A CURLY-COATED kitten was born in an otherwise normal litter at a farm in Cornwall, south-west England. Microscopic examination by a geneticist of the kitten's hair samples showed they were similar to those of the Rex rabbit. When the red and white kitten, named Kallibunker, matured, he was mated with his mother, and two of the resulting three kittens had Rex coats. The male, Poldhu, eventually sired a stunning Rex female called Lamorna Cove, which was exported to the United States to found the Cornish Rex breed on the other side of the Atlantic. British Shorthairs and Burmese cats were used as foundation stock in the early days of Cornish Rex breeding, and eventually there were sufficient curly-coated cats to establish an acceptable breed which could be registered. In Britain, the Cornish Rex achieved full breed status in 1967; in the United States, in 1979.

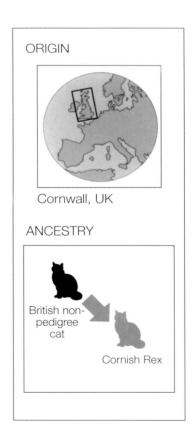

ORIGIN

Cornwall, UK

ANCESTRY

British non-pedigree cat

Cornish Rex

CORNISH REX

In order to widen the gene pool and to ensure stamina in the Cornish Rex as a breed, it was necessary for the pioneer breeders to outcross to other breeds having the desired conformation. Foreign breeds were selected in the main, including Havana and Oriental lilac, and Burmese as well as Siamese of various colours. All the offspring of Cornish Rex to non-rexed cats resulted in cats with normal coats, all carrying the recessive gene for the Cornish curly coat, and when such cats matured, and were mated with similar cats, or back to Cornish Rex, curly-coated kittens were produced. The various colours and coat patterns of the cats selected for the original outcrosses resulted in a wide range of colour varieties in the Cornish Rex breed, and breeders soon began to show their preferences for certain colours and combinations of colours.

All colour and patterns are recognized in the Cornish Rex; the eye colour should complement the coat colour. Those with Siamese point patterns are referred to as Si-Rex.

The fur of the Cornish Rex is curly, fine and silky. The body is long and slender with a constant slight to advanced arch in the back and curl in the long, thin tail. The legs are very long and thin with small, egg-shaped paws. The head is wedge-shaped with a well developed nose and muzzle, medium, egg-shaped eyes and large ears that are pointed.

The Cornish and Devon Rex are affectionate, energetic cats that enjoy gentle play and can even be mischievous in creating their own games.

Black, Smoke and White Cornish Rex

The tail of the Cornish Rex is long, fine and tapered and must be well covered in fur.

Red Cornish Rex

The Cornish Rex is medium-sized, lithe and muscular with long slender legs and small oval paws.

RUSSIAN BLUE

A UNIQUE FEATURE of the Russian Blue is its short, plush, silky coat in a bright, even blue colour, with silver-tipped guard hairs. For contrast, it has striking green, almond-shaped eyes that slant towards the nose, and mauve nose leather and paw pads.

The Russian Blue is a medium Oriental-type, leggy, with a long, slim neck and tail and a graceful body. Its wedge-shaped head bears substantial whisker pads, large ears and a strong chin.

Common faults are obesity, wide head, spots, patterns and white hairs. They are tranquil, affectionate and intelligent cats. Because they like calm surroundings, they prefer families without rambunctious children and unnecessary noise. They are also loving towards each other and make good parents. Although they prefer an indoor life and love to sit by the fire, they can also withstand the cold, as did their Russian ancestors.

The Russian Blue is said to have been introduced to Europe in the 1860s by British sailors visiting the port of Archangel on Russia's northern seaboard. They have also been known as 'Archangel Blues', 'Maltese Blues', 'Spanish Blues', 'Chartreuse Blues', 'British Blues' and even 'American Blues'. They finally acquired their current name in the 1940s because similar cats originated in Russia.

It was shown in Great Britain around the turn of last century when all shorthaired blue cats competed in one class, whatever their body type. In 1912, separate classes were established for British and Russian Blues. After World War II, Scandinavian as well as British breeders began developing Russian Blues, crossing them with British Blue or Blue Point Siamese, which resulted in a new standard reflecting a more foreign body and a new voice. In 1965, some British breeders began returning the breed to its original conformation, and the next year the standard was changed again.

Russian Blues are a challenge to breed because if the coat is correct, there is usually some other fault. And if a Blue lives in a warm climate, it loses its coat and becomes much lighter in colour.

ORIGIN
Russia

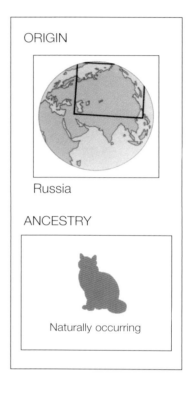

ANCESTRY

Naturally occurring

Coat colour bright blue.

Coat pattern/type short, silky fur.

Eye colour green.

Build medium Oriental-type, wedge-shaped, large ears.

Character tranquil, affectionate and intelligent, prefers calm surroundings.

Care needs a varied diet and regular brushing.

Special problems obesity, wide head, spots, patterns and white hairs.

SCOTTISH FOLD

THE FIRST THING you notice about a Scottish Fold is that its ears are folded forward. Historical chronicles refer to a cat with forward-falling ears taken to Europe from China by an English sailor in the 1880s. It was greeted with interest because, until that time, all known cats in the world had erect ears.

Cats with forward ears resurfaced in 1961 on a farm in Perthshire, Scotland. A shepherd, William Ross, adopted one of the kittens, a white female named Snooks, and registered her. It is not known whether these 20th-century cats had any connection to those in 19th-century China.

American and Australian organizations have given the Scottish Fold full recognition, but British and European groups have not – as they feel that the folded ear is undesirable because it could promote ear mites and impaired hearing. Most experts, however, say that the folded ears cause no discomfort or disability. Nevertheless, British breeders have had to register overseas, and now there are more Scottish Folds bred in the United States than in Britain. They were registered by the CFA in 1974 and received championship status in 1976.

Folded ears come from a single, dominant gene, but unfortunately they are sometimes linked with a deformity in which the legs and tail are thickened. The tail thickening was at first considered desirable, but because the leg thickening interfered with the normal gait, they are now regarded as undesirable traits.

The Scottish Fold should have a wide head, short neck, round eyes, large nose and flexible tail. The short, dense coat may be in any of the recognized colours of the American Shorthair. Eye colour, which should match the coat, can be gold, green, hazel or blue-green. Faults are erect ears, small head and a thick, short or kinked tail.

A remarkable mouser, the Scottish Fold also hunts other small animals. Scottish Folds become attached to only one member of the household but enjoy the company of the whole.

Folded ears cannot be detected on kittens until they are at least a month old.

Coat colour as American Shorhair.

Coat pattern/type short, dense fur.

Eye colour to match coat.

Build short, muscular with wide head, large nose, ears folded forward.

Character affectionate and tolerant of other pets, hardy and able mouser.

Care regular brushing; check and clean ears.

Special problems kinked tail, erect ears, small head.

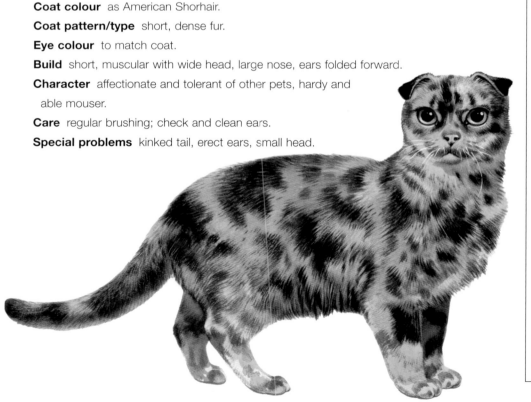

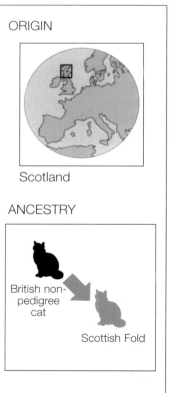

ORIGIN

Scotland

ANCESTRY

British non-pedigree cat

Scottish Fold

BRITISH SHORTHAIR

Coat colour various.

Coat pattern/type short and dense.

Eye colour various.

Build stocky, muscular body, short legs, large round paws, short tapered tail, broad head, large eyes, rounded ears.

Character an excellent family pet, intelligent, affectionate, easy to look after and less excitable than some breeds.

Care easy to feed and groom.

ORIGIN

UK

ANCESTRY

Best of non-pedigree cats

British Shorthair

A NATURALLY OCCURRING type on the streets of Great Britain's cities and towns, the British Shorthair was refined into a recognized breed near the close of the 19th century. Breeders, who admired the intelligence and health of the cat, began to breed the 'best'. The cat is generally healthy, strong, smart and a skilled mouser. It can adapt to virtually all situations, but generally appears happiest when allowed some time outdoors. The British Shorthair quickly comes to love all who show it affection, especially children.

There are many varieties, sharing the same general physical characteristics. The fur is short but dense. The body is stocky and muscular with short, muscular legs and large, round paws. The tail is short, tapered and rounded at the tip. The head is proportionately large and round, with a short nose and a well-defined chin. The eyes are round and large, and the ears are medium and rounded at the tips.

The White British Shorthair has three varieties: blue-eyed (often deaf), orange-eyed and odd-eyed. Black British Shorthairs are coal black with copper, gold or orange eyes.

BRITISH SHORTHAIR

British Blue

The British Blue is by far the most popular and best known of the British Shorthairs. Its large round and glowing eyes of copper, orange or gold perfectly complement the even blue coat.

The Cream British Shorthair is extremely rare, especially perfect specimens, because of the tendency for tabby patterns to accompany its cream colour. The first of this variety appeared in tortoiseshell litters late in the 19th century, but it wasn't until 1920 that the intricacies of purposefully breeding for it were developed and the variety was officially recognized.

Blue British Shorthairs, with copper or orange eyes, appear identical to the Chartreux from France. Although some experts claim that the Chartreux is greyer in colour, the two are generally placed in the same class in US and British shows. The Chartreux is said to have been bred by the Carthusian monks.

The Blue-Cream British Shorthair combines the blue and cream colours from which it was developed in a smoothly intermingled mix. It is almost always a female. The eyes are copper, orange or gold.

There are two tabby patterns. The Classic pattern has three stripes running along its back, a spiral on each flank, and two stripes across its chest like necklaces. Its forehead bears the letter 'M'. The Mackerel pattern resembles that of the tiger. It has more stripes than the Classic and no spirals on its flanks. Either pattern can occur in one of three varieties: brown, silver or red.

Tortoiseshell British Shorthairs have black coats with patches of cream and red. A variety of this type is the Tortie-and-White, which also has white patches.

The Smoke British Shorthair can occur in either black or blue topcoats over a white undercoat. Tipped British Shorthairs are the result of complicated selective breeding, giving a cat with a coat tipped in any recognized colour.

COLOURPOINT SHORTHAIR

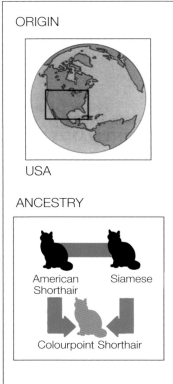

ORIGIN

USA

ANCESTRY

American Shorthair

Siamese

Colourpoint Shorthair

THE FIRST SIAMESE had fawn-colour coats and seal-brown points on their ears, face, mask, legs, feet and tail. Later it was mixed with chocolate, lilac and blue points, which were accepted in the breed in the United States.

Many believe that these are the only true Siamese. When they were crossed with Abyssinians and other shorthairs to achieve more colours for points, the American organizations felt that they should be classed separately because of their non-Siamese genes. Thus was created the Colourpoint Shorthair.

In Britain, the GCCF calls them red points, tabby points (in varying hues) and tortie points (in several colours).

Coat colour red-point, tabby-point, tortie-point.

Coat pattern/type points as for Siamese.

Eye colour clear blue.

Build medium size, lanky, long legs, long and triangular head.

Character highly intelligent, extrovert, enjoys human company and will walk on a leash, long lived.

Care daily grooming; diet should include fish, vegetables and meat.

Special problems non-blue eyes, spotting, malformed tail and weak legs.

COLOURPOINT SHORTHAIR

Many new colours and patterns have been developed recently within the Siamese range. A British seal point Siamese was mated in 1960 with a tabby to produce a single tabby among the seal points. When the tabby was mated back to a seal point, four of the kittens had tabby points. This new breed was recognized by the GCCF and the CFA several years later, and was called tabby point Siamese in Britain and lynx point in America.

Besides the four basic point colours, the Colourpoint is bred in red point, red tabby point, cream point, cream tabby point, seal tortie point, seal tabby point, chocolate tortie point, chocolate tabby point, lilac cream point, lilac tabby point, torbie point, blue tabby point and blue cream point.

A new variety of Colourpoint Shorthair is the silver, called silver tabby point and silver blue tabby point. A silver tabby point Siamese, still relatively rare, has a paler body coat than do other Siamese and is silver between the tabby stripes.

Other than the colouring, the Colourpoint Shorthair carries through the characteristics of the Siamese. It's an extrovert that enjoys all people who give it the attention it demands. It can become a dedicated companion and can be taught to walk on a leash like a dog. The Colourpoint Shorthair also can become jealous of all creatures that compete with it for attention. It has the same loud voice as the Siamese and is just as willing to use it.

The fur is Siamese-like: short, soft and fine. The body is thin and slender, with long, thin legs and small, egg-shaped paws. The head is large and triangular, with medium-sized, almond-shaped eyes that are slanted, and it has a pointed muzzle. The ears are large and pointed at the tips.

Common standard faults are non-blue eyes, spotting on the underside, malformed tail, malformed chin, weak legs and white feet.

Seal Tortie Point

In the Seal Tortie Point the points are a mixture of black and red or light red, and the cat, like this one, may have a red or light red blaze down the face.

SIAMESE

By 1892, the first Siamese breed standard had been written, describing it as 'curious and striking, of medium size, if weighty not showing bulk, as this would detract from the admired, svelte appearance. In type, in every particular the reverse of the ideal shorthaired domestic cat, and with properly preserved contrasts in colours, a very handsome animal, often distinguished by a kink in the tail'.

The kink eventually became a fault, but not before the first champion in Britain, complete with kink, had been named: Wankee born in Hong Kong in 1895. Some early cats also had the squinty, or crossed, eyes, which have been bred out.

Partly because of its personality, the Siamese became fashionable in the 1920s. Unfortunately, breeders could barely keep up with demand and took shortcuts that nearly wiped out the breed.

The Siamese line recovered, but was ravaged in the 1960s and '70s by feline leukaemia virus. It has since recovered again.

Since the 1902 revision of the original standard, the Siamese has evolved into a more sleek and elegant animal than was the original version. The females reach adolescence sooner than those of other breeds and start calling at five months. Even so, they should not be mated until their ninth month. Born almost white, the kittens develop their final colouring gradually. Their eyes, too, change from light to brilliant blue.

Siamese are highly intelligent, loving, independent, talkative and sometimes unpredictable. They demand a great deal of attention and become jealous if they don't get it. They may become attached to one member of the household and take separation very hard. Although they won't come to heel, they enjoy walking on a leash.

There are only four recognized breeds in North America:

Seal Point, with beige coat with seal-brown points;

Chocolate Point, with snow white coat with milk-chocolate points;

Blue Point, with snow white coat with grey points;

Lilac Point, with snow white coat with pink-grey points.

Seal Point Siamese
The original colour, once known as the Royal Cat of Siam. This cat has a pale fawn body and dark seal-brown points which may appear to be black.

SIAMESE

Chocolate Point Siamese
The Chocolate Point has an ivory body and points of a warm milk chocolate.

In Great Britain, the Tabby Points, Tortie-Tabby Points, Tortie Points (in all their colours), Red Points and Cream Points are also officially recognized as Siamese, but in America these are classed as a separate breed: the Colourpoint Shorthairs.

The fur of the Siamese is short, very soft and exceedingly fine. The body is thin and slender, with long, thin legs and small, egg-shaped paws. The head is large and triangular, with medium-sized, almond-shaped eyes that are slanted; it has a pointed muzzle. The ears are large and pointed at the tips. Common standard faults are non-blue eyes, spotting on the underside, malformed tail, malformed chin, weak legs and white feet.

Daily brushing with a medium-hard brush is recommended to remove dead hairs, especially during shedding periods. An exclusively meat diet tends to damage the light colours of the coat, so fish and cooked vegetables should be used alternately with meat. Vitamin supplements are also advisable.

Blue Tabby Point Siamese
Originally called Lynx Points, Tabby Point Siamese were produced by breeders entranced by a litter of kittens which resulted from a mis-mating.

BRITISH TABBY SHORTHAIR

Coat colour various.

Coat pattern/type short, dense coat with clearly defined markings in either classic, mackerel or spotted.

Eye colour various.

Build stocky, muscular body, short legs, large round paws, short tapered tail, broad head, large eyes, rounded ears.

Character an excellent family pet, intelligent, affectionate, easy to look after.

Care easy to feed and groom.

THE BRITISH TABBY SHORTHAIR comes in three coat patterns: classic, mackerel and spotted. All three models exist in a variety of colours: silver, red, brown, cream and blue.

The word 'tabby' is said to come from a type of ribbed skin or taffeta that was developed in an area of old Baghdad known as Attabiya. It is believed that all domestic cats once had tabby markings and, if all those alive were allowed to mate freely, eventually only tabby cats would survive.

All three tabby types, classic, mackerel and spotted, have the letter `M' marking on their forehead, said to stand for the prophet Muhammad, from when he embraced the cat. The classic tabby pattern is also called marbled or blotched. It includes 'necklaces', 'bracelets' and 'rings' on the tail. A line runs unbroken from the corner of each eye, with three stripes running down along the spinal column.

The mackerel tabby looks more like a tiger, even though it is named after a fish. It has a series of narrow lines running vertically down the spine, and fine lines running outwards from the eyes towards the shoulders. The lips and chin should be the same colour as the rings on the eyes. The back of the back paw should be black, the nose should be red and the eyes either orange or copper.

The spotted tabby goes back to Ancient Egypt. The spotted effect is caused by breaks in the classic tabby lines. The spots should be distinct and numerous, forming round, oval or rosette shapes.

A line runs from the corner of each eye to behind the head, and a stripe runs down the spine. There should be a double row of spots on the underside.

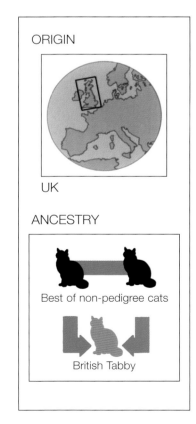

ORIGIN

UK

ANCESTRY

Best of non-pedigree cats

British Tabby

BRITISH TORTOISESHELL SHORTHAIR

Coat colour black, red and cream.

Coat pattern/type short and dense, equally balanced all over body, brilliant and free from blurring.

Eye colour gold, orange or copper.

Build stocky, muscular body, short legs, large round paws, short tapered tail, broad head, large eyes, rounded ears.

Character good family pet, easy to look after, intelligent.

Care should be groomed occasionally with a gloved hand, no special dietary requirements.

Special problems unequal, white or tabby markings.

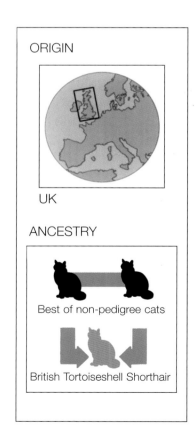

ORIGIN

UK

ANCESTRY

Best of non-pedigree cats

British Tortoiseshell Shorthair

BRITISH TORTOISESHELL SHORTHAIRS (affectionately called 'Torties') are most often female because sex and colour are genetically linked.

The few males that are born are genetically infertile. In the United States, Tortoiseshell and White cats (as well as the British White Shorthairs) are also called calico.

The coat should be black and vibrantly patched with red and cream, and may have a red or cream blaze on the head. There should be some white on the paws, but always more coloured patches. Nose leather and pads should be pink, black or both. Eyes should be copper or orange. When shows began in the late 19th century, the Tortie was among the first to be exhibited. It is even-tempered, intelligent and affectionate.

MALAYAN

Coat colour blue, platinum, and champagne.

Coat pattern/type solid colour, short, fine and soft coat.

Eye colour yellow.

Build stocky, muscular body, large round paws, round head with large rounded ears.

Character very friendly, outgoing, likes lots of attention, like to travel.

Care groom daily with gloved hand, plenty of play and exercise in daily routine.

Special problems wrong colour eyes, kinky tail and white spots.

A RECENT BREED, strictly American, the Malayan was officially recognized only in 1980. It is a twin of the Burmese, differing only in colour. Since they share the same genes, they also have the same inquisitive personality. They are athletic, affectionate, brave, sometimes bossy and very social.

In the United States only the sable-coloured cats are recognized by the CFA as true Burmese, while cats of three other colours are classified as Malayan: champagne, blue and platinum. In Great Britain and elsewhere, all cats of Burmese ancestry and form are labelled Burmese. There, colours other than sable are also recognized, namely red, cream and tortoiseshell (various).

The show standards for Malayans, as well as for American Burmese, differ from those in Britain, Europe, Australia and New Zealand. Americans prefer more rounded heads and eyes, whereas fanciers in other countries like wedge-shaped heads and more oval eyes. Malayans and Burmese in all countries have golden eyes.

Although Malayans are registered separately, they can be born spontaneously of Burmese parents. This is because they are descended from the same cat – Wong Mau. Faults commonly found in this breed include blue or green eyes, a kinky tail and white spots or streaks.

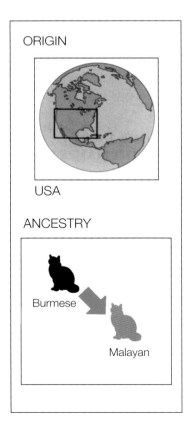

ORIGIN

USA

ANCESTRY

Burmese

Malayan

MANX

THE MANX BREED has two distinguishing features. The more obvious is its 'lack' of a tail. The second is that its hind legs are shorter than its front, leading to a rabbit-like walk.

Manx kittens are divided into four groups, depending on how little or how much tail they bear. The true exhibition Manx, known as a 'Rumpy', has no tail at all, and may have a dimple instead. 'Rumpy-risers' have a few tail vertebrae, in the form of a little knob.

'Stumpies' have a short tail, maybe curved or kinked, and usually movable. 'Longies' have a tail that is only slightly shorter than the norm.

All of the above may be registered as Manx cats, but only the Rumpies may be exhibited – although rumpy-risers without a visible stump are allowed in a few associations. Even though they are barred from exhibiting, the last three categories

Coat colour all colours.

Coat pattern/type solid, bicolour, tabby, calico, marbled and tortie; plush double coat with a cottony undercoat.

Eye colour to suit colour of coat.

Build rounded rump, head and muzzle, rump higher than shoulders.

Character friendly, intelligent, easy to train, home lover but also good hunter, quick reflexes, long lived.

Care groom daily with gloved hand, plenty of play and exercise in daily routine.

Special problems spina bifida is a common problem; raising the vitamin B in the diet of the pregnant queen helps counteract this.

ORIGIN

Isle of Man, UK

ANCESTRY

Naturally occurring

BRITISH BICOLOUR SHORTHAIR

MANY PETS APPEAR to be of this variety grouping of the British Shorthair, but in reality the true pedigree is far from common. In pedigrees the white patches should make up one third and not more of the coat. A symmetrical arrangement is preferred with patches of colour on the top of the head, ears, cheeks, back, tail, legs and flanks.

The common, demanding life on the streets of the breed's ancestors serves the cats well. They are generally healthy, strong and smart. Skilled mousers, they are able to fend for themselves. They adapt to virtually all situations, but are generally active and happy in homes that allow them some time outdoors. They are affectionate to everyone who treats them well and tolerant and loving towards children.

There are four varieties, sharing the same general physical characteristics. The fur is short but dense. The body is stocky and muscular with short, muscular legs and large, round paws. The tail is short, tapered and rounded at the tip. The head is proportionately large and round, with a short nose and a well-defined chin. The eyes are round and large, and the ears are medium and rounded at the tips.

The four colours recognized are British Cream-and-White Bicolour Shorthair, British Orange-and-White Bicolour Shorthair, British Black-and-White Bicolour Shorthair, and British Blue-and-White Bicolour Shorthair. All have copper or orange eyes.

Occasional rubbing with a gloved hand is recommended to keep the fur in its prime. Meat is the staple for a generally wide-ranging, non-restrictive diet. Hair that is too long or shaggy, and irregular noses or tails are common standard faults of the breed.

Coat colour cream/white, orange/white, black/white and blue/white.

Coat pattern/type short and dense, symmetrical blocks of colour.

Eye colour orange or copper.

Build stocky, muscular body, short legs, large round paws, short tapered tail, broad head, large eyes. rounded ears.

Character as with all the British Shorthairs, healthy, hardy, independent, skilled mouser, home-loving, affectionate and good with children.

Care should be groomed occasionally with a gloved hand, no special dietary requirements.

Special problems irregular nose or tail.

ORIGIN

UK

ANCESTRY

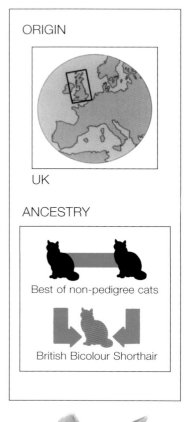

Best of non-pedigree cats

British Bicolour Shorthair

BURMESE

Coat colour brown only in US; also red, cream, blue, lilac, chocolate and tortoiseshell varieties in UK.

Coat pattern/type short, glossy, satin texture, solid colour.

Eye colour yellow or gold.

Build medium-sized, long body, head rounded on top between wide-set ears, straight medium-length tail.

Character highly intelligent, active, sometimes strong willed, affectionate.

Care daily grooming to maintain glossy coat, supplement with vitamins, exercise and play important in daily routine.

Special problems white markings, blue eyes, kinked tail.

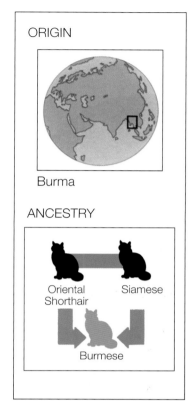

ORIGIN

Burma

ANCESTRY

Oriental Shorthair — Siamese

Burmese

NEARLY ALL MODERN pedigree Burmese cats can be traced back to one walnut-brown female, Wong Mau. She was taken from Rangoon to San Francisco in 1930 by Dr. Joseph Thompson, a US Navy psychiatrist.

Thompson started the first pedigree breed to be developed completely in the United States. Because there were no similar cats with which to mate Wong Mau, Thompson arranged a mating with her closest cousin, a Siamese.

Then he crossed the offspring and Wong Mau. All Wong Mau's kittens were hybrids. When mated back to her, brown kittens resembling their mother were the result. Thus began the Burmese line.

During the 1930s and early '40s, to reduce inbreeding, breeders imported several more Burmese cats from Burma. There were also some outcrossings to Siamese. The Burmese was first officially recognized by the CFA in 1936 and by the Governing Council of the Cat Fancy (GCCF) in 1952. But because the outcrossings with Siamese created too strong a

Siamese look, the CFA suspended registration during the 1940s and '50s. The breed is now well established in Europe, Australia and New Zealand.

Burmese cats have coats like polished mahogany in the United States, but British standard recognizes them in many other colours: red, cream, blue, lilac, chocolate and tortoiseshell (various). All types have yellow or gold eyes which are slanted at the top and rounded at the bottom. They are medium-sized, long, graceful and muscular cats, with long necks, round chests, slender legs and slightly tapering tails. Their heads are rounded on top between their wide-set ears.

The muzzle is shorter than that of the Siamese, with a strong chin and jaw. Faults commonly found in Burmese cats include white marks under the throat, lines or bars on the coat, green or grey eyes, and too dark a colouration.

All Burmese have happy dispositions and make excellent companions. Burmese generally live longer than other breeds, surviving into their middle teens.

BURMILLA

AN ACCIDENTAL MATING between a lilac Burmese female and a Chinchilla Silver male in 1981 resulted in the birth of four black shaded silver female kittens. All were of foreign conformation, and had short dense coats. They looked so spectacular and caused so much interest that similar matings were carried out.

In 1983, the Cat Association of Britain accepted breeding programmes and a standard of points for the breed to be known as Burmilla, to be developed as a shorthaired silver cat of medium foreign type, showing a striking contrast between the pure silver undercoat and the shaded or tipped markings. FIFe granted international breed status to the Burmilla in 1994.

This elegant cat is of medium foreign type with a muscular body, long sturdy legs and a moderately thick, long tail. The head is a medium wedge, with large ears, a short nose and large expressive eyes. Its most impressive feature, however, is the sparkling shaded or tipped ('shell') coat. The ground colour is pure silver white, with shading or tipping in any of the recognized solid or tortoiseshell colours, which must be uniformly distributed. The eyelids, lips and nose leather are rimmed with the basic colour, and delicate tracings of tabby markings are present on the points, which are more clearly defined on the shaded Burmilla.

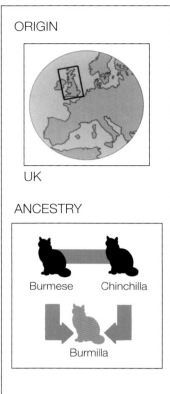

ORIGIN

UK

ANCESTRY

Burmese   Chinchilla

Burmilla

Coat colour shaded or tipped in the following colours: black, blue, brown, chocolate, lilac, red, cream, red tortoiseshell, blue tortoiseshell, brown tortoiseshell, chocolate tortoiseshell, lilac tortoiseshell.

Coat pattern/type short and dense with a silky texture; with sufficient undercoat to give a slight lift to the coat.

Eye colour green or amber.

Build medium-length body with a straight hack and rounded chest, neat oval paws, medium to long tapered tail, large well set apart eyes, medium to large ears.

Character easy going and relaxed, has a playful nature and is very affectionate.

Care should groomed occasionally with a gloved hand, no special dietary requirements.

CHARTREUX

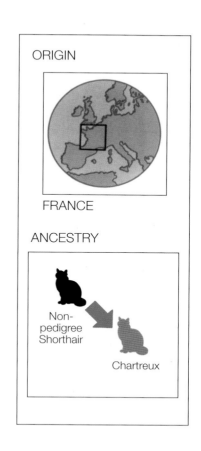

ORIGIN

FRANCE

ANCESTRY

Non-pedigree Shorthair

Chartreux

NATIVE TO FRANCE, the Chartreux is said to have been bred exclusively by Carthusian monks as long ago as the 16th century. The monks lived in the monastery near the town of Grenoble, world famous for its unique liqueur, known as Chartreuse. The naturalist Georges Louis Buffon's work *Histoire Naturelle*, published in 1756, records details of the self-blue feline, and in the 1930s a French veterinarian suggested that the breed should have its own scientific name *Felis catus cartusianorum*.

Today's Chartreux should not be confused with the British Blue or the European Shorthaired Blue. It is massively built, with a very distinctive jowled head, more pronounced in the male than in the female, and is a blue-only breed.

Coat colour any shade of blue from pale blue-grey to deep blue-grey, paler shades preferred, uniform tone essential.

Coat pattern/type dense and with slightly woolly undercoat; double coat makes the hair stand out from the body; glossy appearance.

Eye colour deep yellow, deep copper.

Build medium to large, firm, muscular, wide head, wide jowls, large eyes, medium length tail.

Character self-assured, intelligent, quiet voice, will happily live an indoor life, affectionate.

Care needs regular combing to keep undercoat in good condition; brushing enhances the way in which the coat stands away from the body, a breed characteristic.

Special problems reddish tinge to coat or any shading or markings.

EUROPEAN SHORTHAIR

Coat colour variety of colours regarded as distinct
breeds.

Coat pattern/type various; short, fine, dense, fur.

Eye colour to match coat.

Build robust, solid, muscular with round head and
rounded ears set well apart.

Character placid, friendly and outgoing, makes a
good family pet, territorial and intolerant of other
cats, able mouser, extremely active, enjoys roaming,
long lived.

Care regular brushing will maintain glossy coat,
enjoys meat and milk.

Special problems reproduces more frequently than
other breeds.

ALL GOOD-QUALITY shorthaired housecats of Europe are grouped together under the name 'European'. Although their exact origin is unknown, they probably descended from the African Wildcat, and were introduced to northern Europe by the Romans about 2,000 years ago. Because it has retained its ancestral traits without interference from breeders and geneticists, the European Shorthair is thought to be the most unadulterated of all the breeds.

Large eyes, coloured to match the coat, are featured on the round head with rounded ears. The body is solid and muscular with hardy legs, round feet and a broad chest. The coat is fine and short.

Recognizing the various genes needed to perfect them, the many colours that are permitted are regarded as distinct breeds: European Black, European White, European Albino, European Cream, European Red, European Grey, European Tabby, European Marbled, European Tortoiseshell, European Tortoiseshell with White, European Blue-Cream and European Bicolour.

European Shorthairs are intelligent, lively and inquisitive, with a natural instinct to hunt mice and other animals. Their personalities vary between breeding programmes, and they can be happy either in a small apartment or on a farm estate.

The female especially attaches herself to the entire family because she enjoys the company. If the females are not carefully monitored during periods of oestrus, however, they can reproduce more frequently and with larger litters than other breeds.

ORIGIN

N. Africa and Europe

ANCESTRY

Best of European non-
pedigree

European Shorthair

EXOTIC SHORTHAIR

Coat colour variety of colours regarded as distinct breeds.

Coat pattern/type various; short, plush, dense, fur.

Eye colour to match coat.

Build short and low-set body, solid, muscular with round head and rounded ears set well apart, thick legs with large paws, short bushy tail.

Character combines the placid, affectionate nature of the Persian with the playful inquisitiveness of the American Shorthair; makes an ideal family pet.

Care gentle brushing will keep the coat in good condition, varied diet of meat, cooked vegetables and giblets.

Special problems flat, uneven coat, short or deformed tail, head that is too small, eyes that contrast with coat colouring.

ANOTHER DESCENDANT OF the American Shorthair is the Exotic Shorthair, although this is a man-made breed rather than a natural mutation. Through selective breeding of Persians and American Shorthairs in the 1960s, this new breed was created to carry the dignified character of the Persian but with the shorter, easier-to-care-for coat of the American Shorthair. For a brief period Burmese were also used in the breeding, but they soon fell from favour.

The Exotic Shorthair inherited portions of its temperament from both parental lines. It is calm, less active and affectionate to the whole family like the Persian and playful, inquisitive and an able mouser like the American Shorthair. This new breed also forms an attachment to its home.

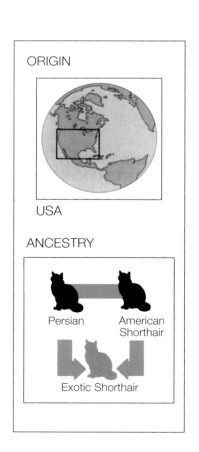

ORIGIN

USA

ANCESTRY

Persian   American Shorthair

Exotic Shorthair

FOREIGN OR ORIENTAL SHORTHAIR

The various colours are divided into five classes: Solid, Shaded, Smoke, Tabby and Bi-colour (Patched).

Coat colours

Solid:

White	white coat and blue, green or yellow eyes
Ebony	black coat and green or yellow eyes
Red	red-brown coat and green or yellow eyes
Lilac (Lavender)	pink-grey coat and green or yellow eyes
Chestnut	brown coat and green eyes
Blue	grey coat and green or yellow eyes

Shaded:

Cameo	white undercoat tipped with red
Silver white	undercoat tipped with black, blue, brown, or pink-grey

Smoke (tipped more heavily than the Shaded):

Black Smoke	white undercoat tipped with black
Blue Smoke	white undercoat tipped with grey
Chestnut Smoke	white undercoat tipped with brown;
Lilac (Lavender) Smoke	white undercoat tipped with pink-grey
Cameo Smoke	white undercoat tipped with red-brown

Tabby: Classic, Mackerel, Spotted, or Ticked (in any of the Tabby colours):

Ebony Tabby	brown coat with black markings
Silver Tabby	silver coat with black markings
Red Tabby	brown-red coat with darker markings
Cameo Tabby	white coat with red-brown markings
Cream Tabby	cream coat with buff markings
Chestnut Tabby	light brown coat with brown markings
Blue Tabby	blue-white coat with grey markings
Lilac (Lavender) Tabby	grey coat with pink-grey markings

Bi-Colour (Patched):

Blue-Cream	grey coat with cream patches
Lavender-Cream	grey coat with cream patches
Tortoiseshell	black coat with red and cream patches
Chestnut-Tortie	brown coat with red and cream patches

The fur of the Foreign Shorthair, like that of the Siamese, is short, very soft and exceedingly fine. The body is thin and slender, with long, thin legs and small, egg-shaped paws. The head is large and triangular, with medium-sized, almond-shaped eyes that are slanted; it has a pointed muzzle. The ears are large and pointed at the tips.

Daily brushing with a medium-hard brush is recommended to remove dead hairs, especially during shedding periods.
An exclusively meat diet tends to damage the light colours of the coat, so fish and cooked vegetables should be used alternately with meat.

The character is identical to that of the Siamese. Demands and gives total devotion. Enjoys travel and will walk on a leash.
Very active and highly vocal. They need lots of play and exercise.

Chocolate Classic Tabby
The classic tabby pattern is shown to perfection by this superbly marked Oriental cat.

HAVANA

Coat colour chestnut brown.
Coat pattern/type solid colour, short fur, very glossy.
Eye colour green or yellow-green.
Build long, thin, Siamese type, wedge-shaped head and round-tipped ears, long tapering tail.
Character intelligent, very affectionate, playful and loyal, demands lots of attention.
Care daily grooming with gloved hand, no special dietary needs.
Special problems marked coat, deformed tail.

ORIGIN

UK

ANCESTRY

Siamese

Havana

THE HAVANA's short brown coat is a rich, chestnut-brown colour, much like the cigar or that of the Havana rabbit, after which the cat is named. It is a variety of Britain's Foreign Shorthair. It bears more resemblance to the Brown Oriental Shorthair of the United States than the Havana Brown, which has a different build. The Havana has a Siamese-type build and green or yellow-green, almond-shaped eyes.

All-brown cats have been treasured for years. Their beauty was celebrated by ancient poets, and they were said to protect people from evil. They arrived early in the West, and were shown to the public in the late 1800s as the 'Swiss Mountain Cat'. In 1930 a solid brown feline appeared, called 'Brown Cat'.

The Havana is the result of a selective breeding programme in the 1950s. The aim, to establish a breed with the graceful build of the Siamese without its pointed coat. The first kitten fulfilling this criterion was from a seal-point Siamese and a short-haired black of seal-point Siamese ancestry.

The breed was first exhibited in 1953, but it was not accepted by the GCCF until 1956, when it was named the Chestnut Brown Foreign. Even so, some thought it too closely resembled the Burmese. Havanas were recognized by the CFA in 1959 as Havana Browns. In the United States, they are judged to the same standard as the Russian Blue, except for the obvious colour distinction.

The British version of the Havana is a Siamese type that looks like the American Oriental Self Brown. The physique of the American Havana Brown is closer to that of the Russian Blue: shorter head and longer fur, and semi-cobby, rather than muscular body.

The Havana likes to sit on people's shoulders and enjoys human company as well as that of other cats. It makes a good housecat, but also appreciates some access to outdoors, such as a terrace or porch. This sleek beauty often investigates objects by touching with its paws, rather than smelling.

The kittens may look like bats because of their large ears and pink noses. Faults are white hairs, hooked tail and spots.

DEVON REX

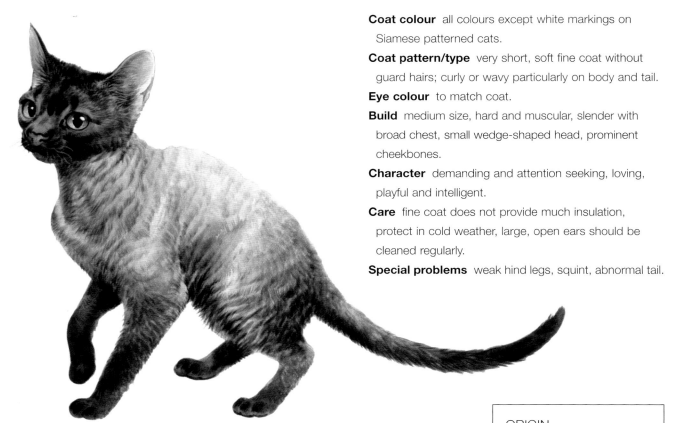

Coat colour all colours except white markings on Siamese patterned cats.

Coat pattern/type very short, soft fine coat without guard hairs; curly or wavy particularly on body and tail.

Eye colour to match coat.

Build medium size, hard and muscular, slender with broad chest, small wedge-shaped head, prominent cheekbones.

Character demanding and attention seeking, loving, playful and intelligent.

Care fine coat does not provide much insulation, protect in cold weather, large, open ears should be cleaned regularly.

Special problems weak hind legs, squint, abnormal tail.

TEN YEARS AFTER the discovery of the first Cornish Rex kitten, another curly-coated kitten was discovered in the neighbouring English county of Devon. The kitten, named Kirlee, was eventually mated with some Cornish Rex queens. To everyone's surprise, all the resulting kittens were flat coated, and it was concluded that Kirlee's curls were caused by a different gene. More breeding tests confirmed this. The gene for the Cornish coat was labelled Rex gene [i]; the gene for the Devon coat Rex gene [ii]. The two rex-coated varieties were developed quite separately, and are quite distinct breeds. The Devon Rex would look rather unusual even without its wavy coat, having a quizzical, pixie-like expression and huge bat-like ears.

In Britain, a popular sub-variety of Devon Rex is known unofficially as the Si-Rex. It combines all of the characteristics of the typical Devon Rex with the Siamese coat pattern and colours.

The Devon is said to be the cat for the connoisseur. It is demanding as a pet, constantly craving human attention, loving, playful and intelligent.

ORIGIN

Cornwall, UK

ANCESTRY

British non-pedigree cat

Devon Rex

DEVON REX

The cat is very easy to groom with hand stroking and occasional combing. It often shows sparse areas on the body, and when it does, the cat needs extra warmth. The large ears need regular cleaning. Whatever their colour or coat pattern, all Devon Rex must conform to the same stringent show standard of points. The coat of the Devon Rex is quite different from that of the Cornish, and in some cats the fur may be sparse and downy on the underparts, often causing the coat colour to look indistinct. Like the Cornish Rex, the first Devons were outcrossed to cats of other Foreign breeds in order to widen the gene pool of available breeding stock. Siamese cats were extensively used and the resulting curled cats were called Si-Rex in the beginning. Si-Rex is not now accepted as correct terminology for the Siamese-patterned Devon Rex, and white markings are not permitted in cats with the Himalayan or Siamese coat pattern, where the colour is restricted to the cat's points.

Apart from this requirement, all colours and patterns accepted in the feline standards are recognized in the Devon Rex, with or without white areas.

Black Smoke Devon Rex
The Devon Rex is totally different from the Cornish. It is of smaller size, but has a unique head type and unusual body conformation.

Chocolate Tortie Point
The Devon Rex appears in a range of Siamese-patterned colours. At one time these were called Si-Rex.

BRITISH SMOKE SHORTHAIR

Coat colour black or blue topcoat over white undercoat.

Coat pattern/type short and dense.

Eye colour orange or yellow.

Build stocky, muscular body, short legs, large round paws, short tapered tail, broad head, large eyes, rounded ears.

Character an excellent family pet, intelligent, affectionate, easy to look after and less excitable than some breeds.

Care easy to feed and groom.

THIS BREED HAS a very unusual coat: a single-colour topcoat over a white undercoat. The topcoat is either black or blue. There should be no tabby or white markings. When the cat moves, a shimmering effect is produced by the layered colours.

This breed was developed in the late 19th century by crossing silver tabby and solid British Shorthairs.

Good-natured, affectionate and smart, it has orange or yellow eyes.

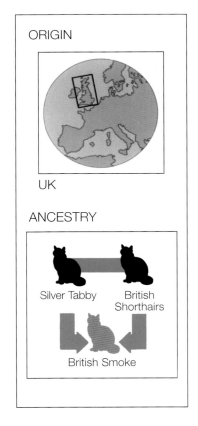

ORIGIN

UK

ANCESTRY

Silver Tabby   British Shorthairs

British Smoke

BRITISH SPOTTED SHORTHAIR

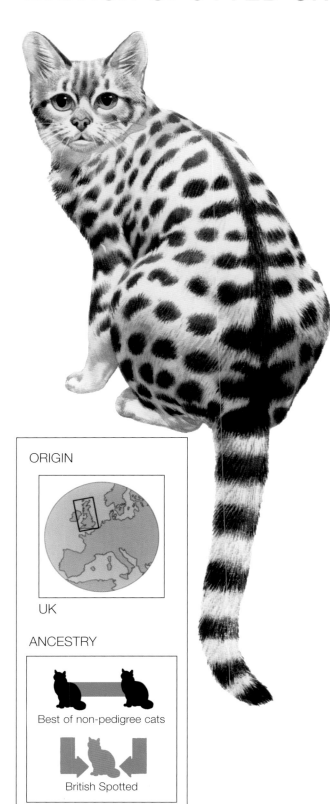

THE BRITISH SPOTTED SHORTHAIR is another group of varieties of the British Shorthair, and as such shares the breed's common beginnings on the street. These cats were among those exhibited at the first shows in Great Britain.

Often referred to as 'Spotties', these cats have the pattern of a Mackerel Tabby British Shorthair, but with the stripes broken up into spots. It is an extremely 'wild' look, resembling the coats of some of the wild cats. For show standards, the spots should be as plentiful and distinct from one another as possible.

Spotting may be any colour accepted for other British Shorthairs, set against an appropriate ground colour, but red, brown and silver are most popular. The brown is light brown with black spots and copper, orange or gold eyes; the red is light red-brown spotted in darker red-brown with orange or copper eyes and the silver is grey spotted in black with green or hazel eyes.

The physical characteristics of the British Shorthair continue in the British Spotted Shorthair. Short, dense fur covers a stocky, muscular body. The legs are muscular and end in large, round paws. The tail is short, tapered, and rounded at the tip. The head is proportionally large and round, with a short nose and a well-defined chin. The eyes are round and large, and the ears are medium and rounded at the tips.

The other characteristics, developed when it was the cat of the streets, are also carried over. The British Spotted Shorthair is healthy, strong and smart. It is a skilled mouser. It also can adapt to virtually all situations, but appears happiest when allowed some time outdoors.

Coat colour various.
Coat pattern/type short and dense, well defined spots.
Eye colour various.
Build stocky, muscular body, short legs, large round paws, short tapered tail, broad head, large eyes, rounded ears.
Character healthy strong and smart, skilled mouser, good with children.
Care should be groomed occasionally with a gloved hand, no special dietary requirements.
Special problems irregular nose or tail, long or shaggy coat.

ORIGIN

UK

ANCESTRY

Best of non-pedigree cats

British Spotted

SINGAPURA

Coat colour ivory ticked with brown or bicolour of white with tabby markings.

Coat pattern/type smooth, close-lying fur.

Eye colour hazel, green or gold..

Build small, muscular, constant slight arch to back round head with short muzzle, very large eyes and pointed ears.

Character placid, undemanding and good-natured, adaptable, enjoys indoor life.

Care groom with gloved hand.

Special problems reserved temperament can be overcome with patient handling.

AS ITS NAME IMPLIES, the Singapura originated in Singapore, where it is the common cat of the streets. It leads a tenuous existence on the small island because human residents there are not particularly fond of cats.

For centuries the small, muscular feline went virtually unnoticed as a distinct breed, until foreigners took an interest in its development. The first Singapura was exported from Singapore to the United States in the mid-1970s, and members of the breed were first shown in 1977. The CFA allows registration of the breed, while most other American organizations accept it for championship status.

Only ivory ticked with brown and a bicolour of white ticked with tabby markings have emerged outside of Singapore at this time, but the cat occurs in many colours and patterns on the island, and some of these can be expected to reach the outside world in the not-too-distant future.

The Singapura retains much from its deprived, streetwise heritage. It is smaller than other domestic cats, with males weighing no more than 2.7 kg (6 lb) and females attaining no more than 1.8 kg (4 lb). It is withdrawn and cautious towards new acquaintances, although it will warm towards anyone who demonstrates that no harm is intended. It reflects this attitude in a perpetually worried look on its face.

The cat sports a smooth, close-lying coat over a small, muscular body with legs of medium length and small narrow paws. Its tail is medium to long and quite straight. The head is round with a short muzzle, firm chin, large pointed ears and very large eyes that are slightly slanted.

Although the Singapura is a street cat by ancestry, it quickly adapts to any environment where it feels cared for. It can develop into an active, playful cat, curious about and involved in the family's every activity.

Owing to its recent 'discovery', the breed remains relatively rare. There is generally a waiting list for kittens, which are very slow to develop.

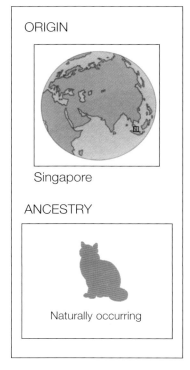

ORIGIN

Singapore

ANCESTRY

Naturally occurring

SNOWSHOE

Coat colour seal point, or blue point.
Coat pattern/type short, fine, close-lying fur, darker markings on legs, tail, face and ears; white paws.
Eye colour blue.
Build medium-sized, well-muscled, long body and strong back, compact oval paws.
Character robust, lively cat, highly intelligent and loving, enjoys human company.
Care groom with gloved hand, no special dietary requirements.

THE SNOWSHOE, so named for its white mittens, is the essence of a modern, man-made breed. It saw its beginnings in a natural mutation that resulted from the crossing of two Siamese cats in the mid-1960s, giving rise to a litter that included three female kittens with white feet. Without a strict breeding programme, such infrequent mutations could have remained the type's only occurrence.

Several American breeders, however, did take a fancy to these beautifully marked cats. They began their efforts by crossing bicolour American Shorthairs with Siamese having white feet, which produced a first generation that was in reality solid or bicolour Oriental Shorthair but registered as Snowshoes. The white-footed bicolours of that first generation were next crossed with Siamese, producing solid, bicolour solid, pointed and bicolour pointed cats. The bicolour pointed cats

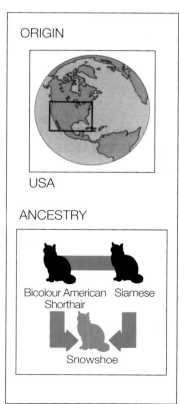

ORIGIN

USA

ANCESTRY

Bicolour American   Siamese
Shorthair

Snowshoe

109

SNOWSHOE

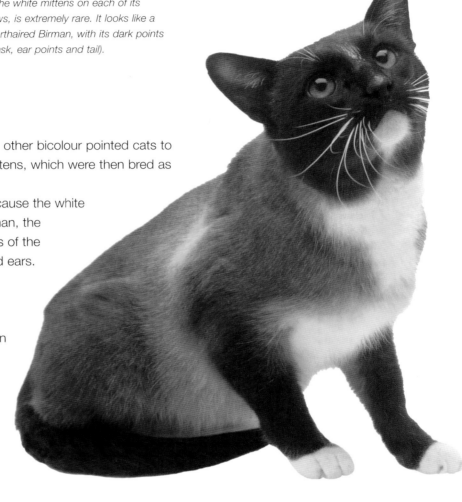

Seal Point Snowshoe
The Snowshoe, so called because of the white mittens on each of its paws, is extremely rare. It looks like a shorthaired Birman, with its dark points (mask, ear points and tail).

with white feet were then bred to other bicolour pointed cats to produce only bicolour pointed kittens, which were then bred as Snowshoe to Snowshoe.

Also called the Silver Lace because the white paws resemble those of the Birman, the Snowshoe retains the dark points of the Siamese on its legs, tail, face and ears. Only two varieties of colours are currently accepted for showing:

Seal Point, which is yellowish- to reddish-brown with dark brown points.

Blue Point, which is bluish-white with dark grey points. The eyes are blue.

The CFA accepted the Snowshoe into championship status in 1983, but many other organizations have yet to recognize the breed.

A smooth, lustrous coat covers a medium-to-large, muscular body with medium legs and a medium-to-long tail. The head is triangular, but not delicate, with large, almond-shaped eyes that are slightly slanted and large, pointed ears.

The Snowshoe is highly people-oriented and will follow members of the family about the house in an ever-present fashion. It hates to be alone and needs a great deal of companionship and attention. Although it lives best as a strictly indoor cat, it remains active throughout its life. Its soft, delicate voice reveals the cat's loving nature. Given its very recent origins as a breed, the Snowshoe remains relatively rare throughout the world.

SPHYNX

ORIGIN

Canada

ANCESTRY

American
Shorthaired → Sphynx

Coat colour all colours are acceptable.

Coat pattern/type all patterns, appears hairless, has some soft down, wrinkled skin.

Eye colour to match coat.

Build long, slender, long tapered tail, elongated triangular head.

Character sociable but dislikes being held A cat for indoors, it prefers peace and quiet.

Care needs a warm environment as it is hairless.

Special problems loose, wrinkled skin, downlike hair on the body, green eyes.

THE SPHYNX is, beyond any argument, the most unusual breed of cat. Unlike every other breed, it is hairless. It is quite rare, and only a few groups officially recognize it for show.

The first Sphynx appeared as a hairless kitten in a litter of otherwise normal, shorthaired kittens in Canada in 1966. Although it is the breed that continues today, this was not the first time that a hairless mutation has occurred. A breed, dubbed the Mexican Hairless, was bred for a short time in Mexico in the late 19th century.

Affectionate and sociable, the Sphynx adapts well to an owner that will respect its desire for peace. It prefers not to be held tightly or cuddled. It should be kept indoors and is best suited to a temperate climate, as it is susceptible to temperature-related illnesses.

Those organizations that recognize the Sphynx accept it in any colour and pattern, with eye colour that complements that of the coat.

The breed is hairless with very fine, black, downlike fur on the face, ears, paws, tail and back. The body is long and slender, made to appear even more so by the lack of hair, with a long, tapered tail. The legs are long and slender, with small, round paws. The head is an elongated triangle, with a short nose, pouty chin, large, almond-shaped eyes and very large, very pointed ears.

TONKINESE

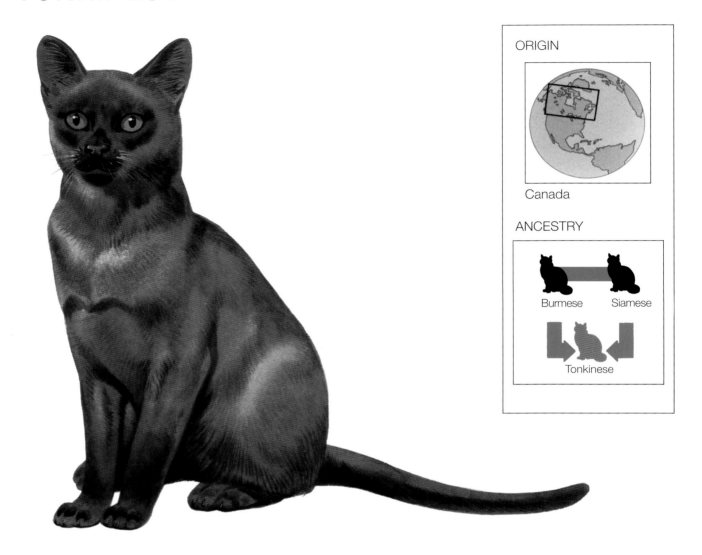

ORIGIN

Canada

ANCESTRY

Burmese   Siamese

Tonkinese

Coat colour natural mink, honey mink, champagne mink, blue mink, platinum mink.

Coat pattern/type darker points as with Siamese.

Eye colour rich blue-green.

Build medium length, with long legs, triangular head with wide-set eyes and rounded ears.

Character outgoing and very affectionate, enjoys exercise and play, adaptable to life indoors and outdoors, travels well and has a long life expectancy.

Care rubbing with a gloved hand keeps the coat shiny, no special dietary requirements.

Special problems loves climbing and can't be trusted with other smaller pets.

ONE OF OUR newest breeds, the Tonkinese originated in the 1970s in Canada, the result of a cross between Siamese and Burmese parents It is a cat with point markings similar to the Siamese, but in the Tonkinese these are much less defined.

It is also one of the most affectionate of cats. Sometimes this affectionate quality can be a liability. Early in its life the Tonkinese associates cars with people, and it has a tendency to stray dangerously close to cars. The cat needs to have its affection returned, both in play and in gentle times together with its owner. It also enjoys exercise outside. The Tonkinese travels very well and enjoys watching the passing landscape.

TONKINESE

It is an extremely active and curious breed, which cannot be trusted near other small pets, such as birds and rodents, even when those other pets are 'safely' confined in their cages. The Tonkinese loves to jump and climb, and is quite willing to do so on trees or on shelves, furniture, curtains and the like. Plenty of exercise is essential to the well-being of this breed. It also thrives on a great deal of attention and tender care, and loves to greet visiting humans into its home.

'Tonks', as some refer to the cats, were registered with the Canadian Cat Association (CCA) in 1974 and the CFA in 1978. Championship status was conferred in 1984. Today, Tonkinese to Tonkinese crosses generally produce a litter that is one-half Tonkinese and one-quarter each of Siamese and Burmese.

The soft, lustrous coat of the Tonkinese looks and feels much like that of the mink and consequently its accepted colours have been given names that reflect this quality. The same colours in other breeds have not been awarded the 'mink' modifier.

There are five varieties all with blue-green eyes:

Natural Mink, brown coat with dark brown markings.

Blue Mink, blue-grey coat with slate-blue markings.

Honey Mink, deep brown coat with chocolate markings.

Champagne Mink, yellow-brown coat with light brown markings.

Platinum Mink, grey coat with darker markings.

Natural Mink
The darkest colour variety with a medium brown coat. As with the other Tonkinese varieties, the eye colour is blue-green.

Platinum Mink
Equivalent to the Lilac Burmese and Lilac Point Siamese, this cat has a pale silvery coat with warm overtones.

TONKINESE

Blue Tortie
*Bluish silver-grey, either patched
or mingled with shades of
cream, produces this pretty
variety.*

Chocolate Tortie
*The introduction of the red or
orange gene into Tonkinese
breeding soon gave rise to an
entire range of tortoiseshells.*

The fur is short, soft and shiny. The body is
medium-sized and slender, with comparatively long legs
ending in small, egg-shaped paws. The head is rounded
with a long nose, a square muzzle, almond-shaped,
slightly slanted eyes and large ears that are rounded
at the tips.

New varieties

Members of the Cat Association of Britain, working
with new colours in Burmese and Siamese cats,
decided to introduce these into the Tonkinese, and the
breeding programmes were provisionally accepted by
CA prior to its becoming the British member of FIFe in
1990. The Cat Association of Britain therefore offers
special awards for Tonkinese in the following colour
varieties: seal, blue, chocolate, cinnamon, lilac, fawn,
caramel, beige, red, cream, apricot, indigo and all these
colours as tortoiseshell, tabby and tortie.

THE COMPLETE GUIDE
TO KEEPING A CAT

ANATOMY & CHARACTERISTICS

Your gentle little Fluffy may not look very fierce curled up on your couch, but she has a digestive tract designed for meat-eating, and the physique and instincts of a hunting animal (one that stalks, pounces and tears). Although dogs and cats are both carnivores, cats are more adapted to the role of hunter. In general, wild dogs hunt in packs, while most cats hunt alone. Because dogs have been companions to humans for so long, they have lost much of their resemblance to their wolf-like ancestors. But cats still retain the physique and temperament of their wild relatives.

The average cat weighs about 4 kg (9 lb), is 30 cm (12 in) high at the shoulder, and about 80 cm (31 in) long from head to tip of tail. Its 245 bones and 517 muscles are formed into one of three basic cat shapes:

cobby	flat face, short legs, wide shoulders and hind, and short, round head.

muscular	medium legs, shoulders and hind, with slightly round head.

lithe	long thin legs, narrow shoulders and hind, and long, wedge-shaped head.

Cats' vertebrae are more loosely connected than are humans', making their spines very flexible – a big plus for squeezing through tiny spaces. This also enables the cat to arch its back. They are good climbers, thanks to the strong muscles in their backs and legs, and the curved claws on their paws. Unfortunately, they are not as adept at climbing down, because their claws curve the wrong way and their powerful muscles aren't adapted to holding back the body's weight. That is why cats sometimes seem inept at coming down a tree once they have climbed up.

Although many cats are wanderers, they don't spend a great deal of time walking. As runners, they are better at short distances than long. When they run, they extend their legs completely in the air, then bring them down and thrust themselves forward from both back feet at once. Their feet are digitigrade (walking on the ends of their toes), as opposed to plantigrade (walking flat on the paw bones), and their forepaws have five toe pads, five claws and two large pads. The fifth claw acts like a thumb, for grasping. The hind paw has four toe pads, four claws and one large pad.

As efficient as the limbs are, it is a myth that cats can jump from high places and always land on all fours. But they can do almost anything connected with their senses. Cats have a greater field of vision than ours, allowing them to make accurate judgements in various terrains: 120 degrees of binocular (straight-ahead) vision, plus 80 degrees of monocular vision on each side, making a total of 280 degrees.

A curious membrane at the back of the eye called the *tapetum lucidum* houses a special light-conserving mechanism that enables cats to make the most of dim light. At night, the pupil opens wide to catch any available light, causing the tapetum to glow in the dark. In bright light, the pupil narrows to a slit. When cats are ill, a greyish membrane called a 'haw' (third eyelid) extends from the eye's edge to protect and moisten the eye.

People sometimes think that cats are psychic because they seem to be able to detect disturbances long before they happen. In reality, they just hear things before we do and things that we cannot hear because of the pitch. Cats can perceive high-frequency sounds up to about 65kHz (65,000 cycles per second). Humans hear up to about 20kHz.

In general, the size of the ear is indicative of the origin of the breed. Ears are an important means of heat loss, and so larger ears would indicate temperate to tropical origins, where they could function as a cooling mechanism. Small ears, like those of Persians, support the theory of a more northerly origin. Possibly because of their well-developed sense of balance, for which the ears are partly responsible, cats do not usually suffer from motion sickness.

The nose and mouth are very closely linked for a cat's sense of smell and taste. A cat's nasal cavity is filled with bony plates called turbinals that increase the surface area for smelling. Despite the small size of the head, a cat has about 60 million scent cells, compared with the 5–20 million present in humans.

In the cat's mouth are 30 teeth (including four canines), which serve to kill and then tear up fresh prey. The rough surface of the tongue, which is loaded with sensory detectors for temperature and taste, is also useful for cleaning fur. Cats are able to taste sour, salt, bitter, sweet and water, but sweetness is not very important to them.

A cat's sense of touch involves its fur and skin, as well as its whiskers. In practical terms, both fur and whiskers are extensions of the skin. The skin includes a great number of 'touch spots' that are more sensitive than the areas around them. On the back of the neck, the skin is very thick and loose, suggesting that cats have not only been hunters but have been hunted themselves. Loose skin makes it easier for animals to squirm away from their captors. The loose skin also helps them work their way through precarious areas.

Fur does not have to actually touch something to feel it. Air flow caused by or bouncing off an object can be enough to alert a cat. But as sensitive as cats are to touch, they are not nearly as sensitive to temperature. Cats are not well adapted to cold or wet weather because they lack the protective layer of fat that dogs have. Whereas humans start to feel pain when touching something at about 44°C (112°F) cats don't notice it until about 51°C (124°F). Fortunately, cats' noses, snouts and upper lips are extremely sensitive to temperature changes. Whiskers, too, called 'vibrissae', act as feelers. They grow on the back of the forelegs, as well as on the face.

At the cat's other end is the tail, a flexible extension of the spine that is just one of the many ways that cats convey their feelings. The tail whips up if the cat is threatening, stands upright and twitches if the cat is alert, and swishes low and close if the cat is aggressive. A raised, still tail is the sign of a friendly cat; an arched, bristled tail, a defensive cat; a thumping tail, a submissive cat. These tail signals are accompanied by signals from the ears, eyes, back and other body parts to convey a variety of feelings and messages.

An aggressive cat also has pricked ears held slightly back, smooth fur, narrow pupils, bristled whiskers and an open mouth. A defensive cat holds its ears back and sideways, bristles its fur and whiskers, arches its back, turns its body sideways, dilates its pupils and holds its mouth open. A submissive cat flattens its ears, fur and whiskers, cringes, dilates its pupils and holds its mouth open. A contented cat sits with eyes half-closed, maybe purring.

RUNNING AND JUMPING

The domestic cat is a lazy animal, and it would much rather find a comfortable spot on your bed, or your favourite chair, than engage in physical effort.

This does not, of course, mean that it cannot do so when it wishes, or when events force it to. As everyone – particularly the unwary mouse or bird – knows, cats are among nature's fastest movers over a short distance.

They are all digitigrade, which means they walk on their toes, rather than the soles of their feet, making them very light of foot. The soft pads, on which the hunting cat can move so stealthily, are also on the toes. The heel bone is well-developed, but is set far back, so that it never touches the ground at all. The pads of the feet form cushions, which act as shock-absorbers, protecting the vital bones on which the cat's weight rests.

Cats cover the ground in a series of giant leaps, and do not run in the same fashion as the dog, or most other animals. They move the front and back legs on one side, and then the front and back legs on the other. The only other mammals to do this are the giraffe and the camel, and these ungainly-looking creatures can hardly be compared with the feline.

The body of the cat has a quite remarkable degree of flexibility. The point of the shoulder is open and free, which allows the animal to turn its foreleg in almost any direction without difficulty. In addition to this, the feline clavicle, or collar bone, is extremely small; in fact some cats do not have one at all.

Cats are finely-tuned physical instruments, beautifully balanced and able to rotate their powerful limbs without the hazard of dislocation. Their overall framework is a masterpiece of elasticity, and this is what makes them so lithe and agile. No part of their bodies is as mobile as the spinal column which allows the tail to bend at will in any direction.

Below The famous series of pictures of the running cat is from Eadweard Muybridge's Animals in Motion. It clearly shows the grace, power and sheer athleticism that make the cat one of the fastest movers over a short distance.

Oddly enough, the only other animals with the same action are the ungainly camel and giraffe. The frame of the cat is a natural masterpiece of elasticity, allowing it to run and jump with ease, using the pads of its feet as shock-absorbers. This protects the bones on which its weight rests.

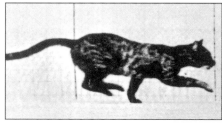

SLEEPING PATTERNS

Any sunny spot will do. Cats like to feel warm and secure before they sleep. They will often change their sleeping pattern with the movement of the sun, to compensate for the slight drop in body temperature when sleeping.

Cats have two distinct types of sleep – light sleep and deep sleep. During light sleep the blood pressure remains normal, the body temperature drops slightly and the muscles are mildly tensed. In deep or paradoxical sleep, the blood pressure falls, the body temperature rises and the muscles relax completely. The hearing, however, remains extremely acute and any sudden sound will wake the cat instantly. Cats seem able to sleep at any time, in any temperature and in all manner of seemingly uncomfortable situations.

Small kittens sleep most of the time, and this is an important part of their development process. Newborn kittens spend most of their first week of life in deep sleep, and during the next three weeks have gradually increasing periods of wakefulness.

Dreaming takes place during deep sleep, and cats often twitch their muscles, growl or purr. They may make sucking sounds and twitch the tail. It is probably during dreaming that the cat's brain sorts and sifts data for storage in its long-term memory. At least one-third of the cat's sleeping time is spent in deep sleep mode, and this seems to be essential for its well-being.

Sleep patterns

As a cat becomes drowsy and falls into a light sleep it may remain sitting or lying with its head up but relaxed, and its paws tucked into its body. It may remain in this condition for 10 to 30 minutes and at this stage it is easy to awaken with any slight noise. In deep sleep the cat is completely relaxed and usually curled on its side. Deep sleep is characterized by rapid eye movements, and the cat may also twitch its whiskers and paws, or quiver the ears, and tail. It may even growl or emit little muttering sounds. Deep sleep normally lasts for about 6 to 10 minutes before the cat resumes a period of light sleep.

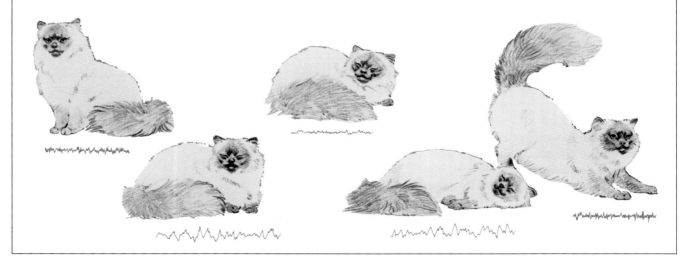

WASHING AND GROOMING

Most cats wash themselves frequently. Family cats often indulge in mutual washing sessions, and mother cats spend a great deal of time washing their young kittens. Pet cats will often attempt to wash their humans, and many cats wash meticulously after being touched or stroked by humans, probably in an attempt to remove an unacceptable scent from their coats.

The cat uses its tongue and paws to groom itself. The tongue, covered with tiny hooked projections called papillae, acts as both brush and comb. Front paws are used to clean the places the tongue cannot reach. The cat sits up and licks a paw until it becomes damp, then passes the paw over its face, over and into the ear, across the forehead and eye and down the cheek to the chin. It repeats the procedure with the opposite paw to clean the other side of the face. It licks and grooms each shoulder and fore leg in turn,

***Above** The cat licks a paw then uses it to wash one side of its face.*

Washing

The cat thoroughly cleans each shoulder and flank.

It washes its underside and inside each hind leg in turn.

The paws are licked and any dirt is bitten from between the paws.

Each forepaw is licked in turn and used to wash the corresponding side of the face and head.

then attends to its flanks and underside, the anus, genital region and hind legs, and finishes by washing the tail from the base to the tip. It teases out tangles and knots with its teeth, and bites out patches of dirt from between its paws.

As well as keeping its coat clean and well groomed, the cat's washing technique has another important purpose. The effect of sunlight on the coat produces its nutritional requirement of Vitamin D, which it transfers from the coat into the body by the licking and washing action.

Below and opposite page *Friendly cats often indulge in mutual grooming of each other's fur, which both seem to enjoy.*

Self-grooming

The first active relationship between mother and newborn kitten is grooming. Within seconds of birth, the mother is using her tongue and teeth to loosen the kitten from its enveloping membrane, stimulate breathing and dry its soaked body.

Within hours, the mother must remove parasites such as fleas. These congregate in dozens around the mouth and eyes of the helpless kitten and, unless the mother is diligent, the kitten's strength will be sapped. Many unfortunate kittens are permanently stunted by fleas which the mother could not control.

Grooming is one of the first activities that the kitten is capable of performing on its own. In one study of 40 kittens under laboratory conditions, the eyes opened at 12 days, walking began at 22 days and grooming a day later.

Kittens reared without their mothers, in separate incubators, began grooming at 15 days, two days before they began walking. It was difficult to evaluate, for the kittens tended to perform sucking movements on their own bodies soon after birth.

Grooming actions are inborn. Some species of rat wash their faces using the palms of both paws. The paws make effective brushes because the palms are flat. The cat cannot use its paws like this, because its claws are too long and the pads too closely set.

It uses its forearms as a brush, and then uses its tongue to clean the forearm. Unlike many smaller animals, the cat uses only one forearm at a time while grooming. Obvious anatomical limitations confine that sort of grooming to the face and head. Most of the grooming of the other parts of the body is done using the tongue alone. The fit cat can assume the most unlikely and seemingly unbalanced postures with an enviably athletic grace and style.

Throughout the entire animal kingdom, the process of grooming occupies only slightly less time than sleeping or even mating.

Furred animals have little option in the matter, for they must constantly strive to keep their covering in the very best condition This is partly for comfort, but its more important function is to maintain its unique qualities of insulation.

One reason for grooming is the sheer pleasure it gives the animal involved. Most cats come to enjoy being groomed by their owners. The areas they particularly enjoy having scratched or stroked are those that they cannot easily reach or deal with themselves.

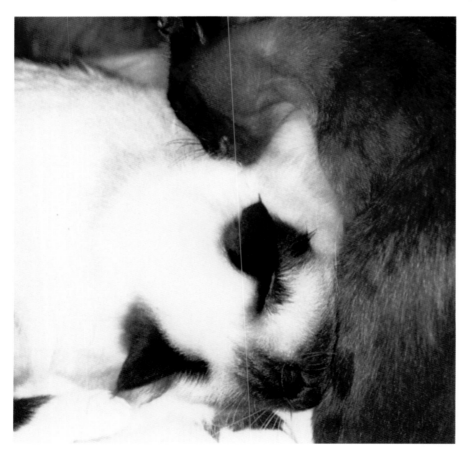

Grooming your cat

The easiest way to groom a cat is to get one that does not need any grooming This is not as facetious as it sounds, for the majority of cats can and do maintain themselves without any human assistance. It would be arrogant to presume that creatures which have managed by themselves for millions of years have, in a mere 5,000 years of domestication, become dependent on man for this essential activity.

The great exceptions are thick-coated and long-haired types which man has encouraged with selective breeding. Perhaps the most beautiful of these are the Angoras, or Persians. Most breeders and lovers of these types proudly admit that it requires at least 30 minutes of daily grooming to keep them in prime condition.

Every vet, boarding cattery and feline beauty parlour will agree that only a few months of neglect can create such a tangled mess that the only method of restoring order is by cutting or clipping off the whole lot. Nor is that an easy task, for the animal often requires a general anaesthetic.

To prevent that situation arising, the owner must get the kitten accustomed to daily grooming from the day of its arrival in the home. As with children, the introduction must be painless and, if possible, pleasurable. Many a cat which has been gently introduced to combing and brushing will eagerly leap onto the table and purr throughout the proceedings, no matter which part of the body is being combed.

There are hundreds of grooming aids on the market, many of them indistinguishable from those used on dogs. The majority of the aids are combs, brushes or gloves. Finely-spaced combs – known in the trade as flea-combs – may be useful in grooming short-coated or silky-coated cats. However, their use is limited on cats with more luxurious coverings, for they tend to glide over the surface without ever penetrating to the layer below. Although they are called flea-combs, it is important to remember that they do not automatically eradicate the target. Unless the flea is trapped and killed, the comb's only function may be to give the parasite a free ride to another part of the body.

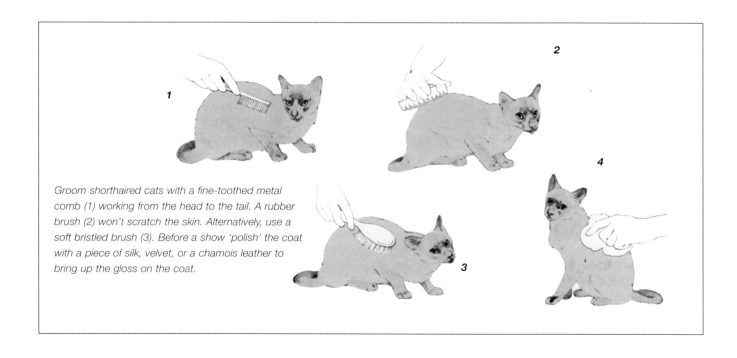

Groom shorthaired cats with a fine-toothed metal comb (1) working from the head to the tail. A rubber brush (2) won't scratch the skin. Alternatively, use a soft bristled brush (3). Before a show 'polish' the coat with a piece of silk, velvet, or a chamois leather to bring up the gloss on the coat.

Before undertaking this painstaking task, the owner should remember that no matter how numerous the enemy, the only really effective way of killing is to focus on one flea at a time.

One of the most useful combs is the one shaped like a garden rake, but with two rows of parallel teeth fairly widely spaced. This tool is so under-rated on the market that many good pet departments and shops do not even bother to stock it. However, it is well worth the effort involved in looking around for one. This invaluable aid can easily and efficiently penetrate and remove dead hairs from the thickest-coated animal.

It is common knowledge that cats do not enjoy taking a bath. Indeed, most of them do not need to, for they will constantly wash themselves. However, even the sure-footed cat can occasionally fall into something that has to be bathed away. In this event, place the cat in two or three inches of water, soap with a shampoo suitable for cats, rinse and repeat. Be sure to keep first aid equipment handy to treat your scratches and other wounds, for your cat can be relied on not to feel the slightest gratitude for your assistance.

Curious cats have been known to fall into the bath. If they get soaked to this extent, they have great difficulty in washing themselves dry. A very gentle going-over with the hair-dryer may frighten a wet cat for a moment, but the creature will soon be basking in new found comfort.

Above Grooming equipment should include a slicker brush (1) for long-haired tails, a wire and bristle brush (2), a wide and fine toothed comb (3) for the coat, and a toothbrush (4) for cleaning the face.

To groom longhaired cats, use a wide-toothed comb (1) to remove debris and tease out mats. Brush some talcum powder or fuller's earth (2) into the coat to add body. Brush out the powder immediately. Use a wire brush (3) to remove dead hair, paying particular attention to the rump. Gently brush the face area with a toothbrush (4). Run a wide-toothed comb through the hair, upwards towards the back, and fluff out the ruff around the neck (5). For show cats, use a slicker brush on the tail.

PHYSICAL FITNESS

Cats are not usually hypochondriacs, and a caring owner should soon notice if there is anything wrong. With a good home, and the exercise provided by some outdoor life, your cat has a good chance of remaining bright-eyed and full of life.

Some possible signs of trouble

Difficulty in walking If your cat appears to have a broken limb, its movement should be restrained. The easiest way of doing this is simply to put the cat into its basket – then take it to the vet. If there is no obvious fracture, check that the cat hasn't got something caught in its paw or claws. If there is tenderness, bathe it in warm salt water.

Toilet difficulties If your cat appears to be constipated, or has difficulty in passing urine, take it to the vet.

Balding patches These may indicate ringworm. Wash your own hands. Avoid handling the cat, and take it to the vet. Cats are also subject to fleas, lice and ticks. You can cope with these yourself, with initial instruction from a vet if necessary.

Worms If you have any suspicions on this count, talk to the vet.

If your cat displays any signs of illness, or any untoward behaviour which might suggest sickness, take it to the vet straight away. No one wishes to bother the vet needlessly, but it is better to be safe than sorry. Some possible signs of trouble are indicated on this page.

Digestive problems If your cat persistently vomits or has diarrhoea, stop feeding it, and take it to the vet.

Ear Problems Many cats scratch their ears, twitch them and shake their heads occasionally, but constant repetition of these actions suggests the presence of ear-mites or some other irritant.

Excessive thirst Do not deny your cat water in these circumstances. If a cat gives the appearance of being thirsty, yet does not drink, this may be a sign of Feline Infectious Enteritis, which is serious.

Eye problems If your cat is feeling 'low', its eyes may shield themselves with an extra eyelid. This may look alarming, but it is a useful warning sign, and will disappear as soon as the cat's ailment has been identified and successfully treated. If the eye is simply water ing, or has a discharge, bathe it with dilute salt water, then take the cat to the vet.

Salivation Cats sometimes salivate when they are expecting a tasty meal, but persistent salivation may indicate poisoning or flu, in which case it is important to see a vet. If your cat has 'bad breath', this may indicate decaying teeth, but it could result from kidney problems.

Coughing Your cat may have something caught in its throat; it may have an allergy; or it may have flu. Persistent sneezing is likely to indicate flu, which is both infectious and dangerous among cats.

THE ARDENT HUNTER

It is easy to distinguish between the cat resting on the lawn and the one paying very special attention to something in the undergrowth. The whole attitude of quivering tension and utter concentration makes it clear that a drama is about to be enacted.

Occasionally a bird or a rodent will fall into the cat's capable jaws, but in the main it must painstakingly stalk its prey before it pounces.

The manner in which it does this, and the time it must spend on it varies considerably, depending on where the cat lives. The majority of cats live in well-tended suburbia, where the rodent population is rigidly controlled by man, and the birds enthusiastically protected.

In this sort of affluent society, the cat may have to spend hours in search of its prey. Sometimes it may spend the best part of a day patiently waiting by a mousehole, or crouched in a tree. The young cat is more likely to persevere, the older one becomes bored. This hunting cat easily becomes a sleeping cat.

The farm cat, or one which operates around factories and the rubbish bins of the modern city centre is more fortunate. For it, the hours of crouching are likely to be reduced to mere minutes.

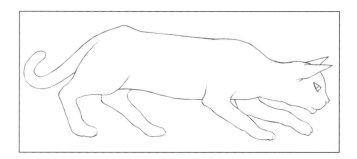

Crouching to kill

Top right *The cat spies its prey and goes into a crouch, waiting for the right moment before beginning the slink-run. Head, body and tail seem to glide along the ground as the cat makes ready for the pounce.*

Middle *Toes dig in, heels rise and the hind legs move back. The tip of the tail reflects this contained energy by twitching. The whole posture is similar to that of a sprinter waiting for the gun. Finally, it pounces, but always keeps at least two feet firmly planted on the ground – just in case it should need a sudden means of retreat.*

Bottom right *The small drama is complete as the cat lands on its unfortunate prey, seizing it with mouth and forelegs. Without assistance from a human, the prey is doomed to die.*

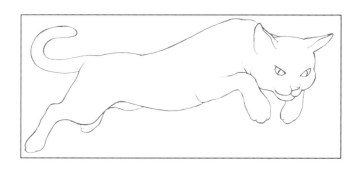

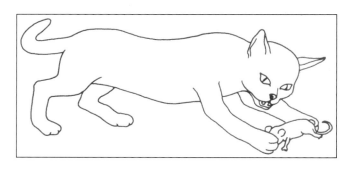

CHOOSING & CARING FOR A CAT

Keeping a cat can be a costly exercise, in terms of food, cat litter and veterinary fees. And yet millions of people throughout the Western world enjoy the luxury of owning a cat. So if you do decide to become a cat owner, you will certainly not be alone. But before you jump in, take a little time to determine if your lifestyle is suited to cat ownership.

Do you have enough time to devote to care and companionship? Although cats do not require as much care as dogs, they still need daily love and attention. Do you have enough room for a cat's needs? Some cats are wanderers at heart, and also need exercise. If they lead a normal, active life, they will get all the exercise they need, exploring, chasing intruders, hunting and being curious. If you live in a flat or apartment or plan to keep your cat inside, choose a breed suited for these living conditions, not one known to prefer wandering. Breeds that do not take to an exclusive indoor life include Somali, Abyssinian and Rex. (See specific breed descriptions for further details). If you live in a congested area, you may want to exercise your cat on a leash. Breeds that will adapt better to a leash than others include Siamese, Burmese, Russian Blue, Colourpoint Shorthairs and Oriental Shorthairs.

Can you afford the food, dishes, collar, leash, licence (if applicable), inoculations, boosters, medical care, bed, toys, grooming tools and other cat paraphernalia? Although you won't need to provide constant entertainment for your cat, you will need to provide it with some basic essentials.

If you answer 'yes' to all these questions, then the next step is deciding which cat is for you. Do you want a pedigree or non-pedigree cat? If you want to try your hand at breeding, you'll need a pedigree. If not, other considerations are more important.

Bear in mind too that a pedigree can involve considerably more financial outlay than an ordinary cat.

(See the earlier section on breeds to determine which breed best suits your lifestyle and needs.)

Where should you obtain your cat? If you want a pedigree, check with local breeders. If not, go to someone who has kittens or the local animal shelter. It's best to stay away from pet shops, where animals sometimes pick up diseases and parasites.

Should you spay or neuter it? In the United States, animal shelters handle approximately 4.5 million felines a year; more than 60 per cent of these are destroyed. So if you are not planning to breed, avoid bringing more unwanted kittens into the world.

Will its claws bother you? Declawing disqualifies a cat from showing in the US and is illegal in the UK. Most experts believe it to be an unnecessary mutilation because claws are trimmed down naturally with exercise. If your cat does not spend much time outdoors, trim its claws regularly as an alternative to declawing. You can also help the natural process by providing a scratching post. Untrimmed claws may grow into the paw pad and cause health problems.

Male or female? Both sexes are affectionate and make good pets, but females in general are more affectionate. Unneutered males spray, wander and may fight; unneutered females have periods of heat and possibly unwanted pregnancies.

Kitten or adult? Kittens need more attention, so an older cat may he better if you plan to be absent during the day throughout the breaking-in period. Kittens are also more energetic, so think twice about acquiring one if your lifestyle would he upset because of that. Kittens, however, find it easier to settle in from the start because they are too young to remember their previous home.

Is the cat healthy? Before you finalize ownership, have a veterinarian check the animal's coat, eyes, nose, ears, mouth, teeth, abdomen and anal area for signs of disease or defects. If the cat passes its medical check, make and keep regular appointments for check-ups, vaccinations and booster shots.

At the time when you acquire your new cat, make sure you have all the necessary equipment: litter box, litter, bed, collar, food dish, food, water bowl, grooming tools and scratching post. Place the food, water, litter and bed in a safe, draught-free place that you think the cat will like. Make sure your house is cat-proof, for the animal's sake as well as for the protection of your valuables and breakables. Take note of whether you have any toxic plants (*Caladium, Dieffenbachia, Euphorbia pulcherrima, Hedera, Nerium oleander,*

Creating a 'cat-safe' environment

Cats are naturally curious, and good climbers; you will need to take some precautions to create a safe home for yourself and for your pet.

Common dangers around the house are:

(A) *doors leading on to high balconies left open.*

(B) *electrical cables which the cat might chew.*

(C) *objects resting on table edges.*

(D) *fragile objects on shelves.*

(E) *poisonous houseplants.*

(F) *fires without fireguards.*

(G) *boiling pans which the cat might spill.*

(H) *open oven doors.*

(I) *accessible rubbish bins containing sharp objects.*

(J) *household cleansers and detergents.*

(K) *boiling kettles.*

(L) *open refrigerators.*

(M) *open washing machines or clothes dryers.*

(N) *sharp utensils left out.*

(O) *drawers left open.*

(P) *babies or young children left alone in a room with a cat.*

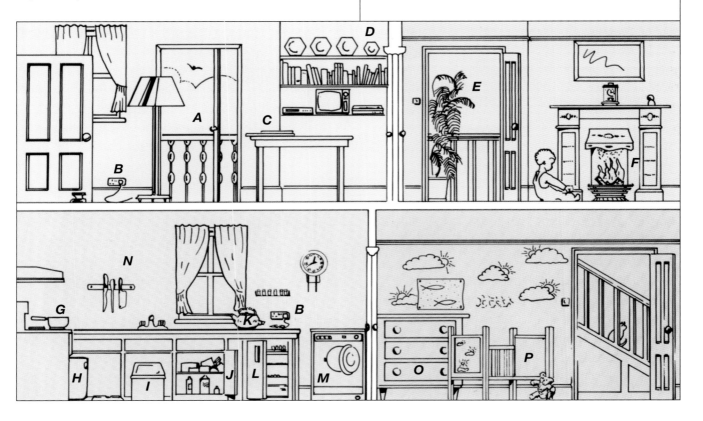

THE INSPIRING SPIRIT

With the spread of Christianity, cat worship declined. Although there is only one reference to cats in the Bible, the animal has played a significant and continuing role in Christian art, particularly painting. A legend in Italy says that at the moment Mary gave birth to Jesus, a pregnant cat, living in the same manger, had a litter of kittens.

This charming tale has influenced many artists, most notably Leonardo da Vinci, who included a cat and kittens as a part of many of his studies of the Madonna and Child.

In 1504 Albrecht Dürer produced an engraving of the Garden of Eden, which showed a cat sitting at the foot of the Tree of Life, its tail curled around Eve's legs. The undoubted virtues of cats have continued to inspire artists throughout the centuries, from Rembrandt to Renoir, and Gainsborough to Gauguin.

Writers and poets have also come under the beguiling spell of the cat. Lewis Carroll created the vanishing Cheshire Cat – illustrated by Tenniel – for *Alice in Wonderland*, while Edward Lear gave the world the whimsical classic tale of *The Owl and The Pussycat*.

Leonardo da Vinci was one of many artists to be fascinated by the Cat, as these studies show (opposite). Above is an ancient Egyptian bronze figurine wearing gold earrings dedicated to the cat-headed goddess Bast, or Pasht, from which the word Puss possibly comes. The Ancient Egyptians revered cats, and killing or eating one of them was an offence punishable by death.

T. S. Eliot revealed himself as one of literature's great cat lovers with his *Old Possum's Book of Practical Cats*.

Just as enduring as any of the great works of art involving the cat, is the central role played by the animal in the development of the cartoon movie culture. *Felix the Cat* was the daddy of all animated felines, and these early productions can still be seen on television. They have an endearing naivety which contrasts sharply with the sophisticated sadism of *Tom and Jerry*, and Sylvester's equally evil attempts to kill Tweetie Pie. It's enough to make a cat laugh.

AND WHEN HE GOES OUT, I'LL GO IN

RATS!! MORNING AND MY SCHEME DIDNT WORK YET

Two enduring felines. Tenniel's famous Cheshire Cat, *which disappeared, leaving Alice with only a smile, was the forerunner of such 'stars' as Felix, the first animated cartoon cat. The frolics of Felix were the inspiration of the modern mayhem carried out by* Tom and Jerry, *and the slightly more sinister Sylvester.*

THE COMMUNICATIVE CAT

Cats are endlessly fascinating creatures. They have occupied a special place in the affairs of man for thousands of years. They have been worshipped and feared, loved and loathed – but never ignored.

The people with whom they share a home are totally committed in their favour. Cat lovers will swear that their animal companions speak to them. They are right, although this rapport is obviously not in the sense that man and cat can exchange a few words on the subject of the weather. Cats are far more subtle than that.

The feline face, often so inscrutable, is capable of great expression. Indeed, almost every thread of the cat's being has a language of its own, as communicative as mere words. Cats have a range of sounds, gestures, rituals and seemingly inflexible habits, which all blend into a subtle and complex pattern of communication. This may not be communication among equals, but it is certainly a dialogue between partners. No sensible human would ever consider for a moment that he actually owns a cat. He and the animal may live in harmony under the same roof, and the man may operate the can-opener at dinner time, but the cat will never look upon him as master. The cat does not really need man at all, although humankind certainly makes feline life a great deal easier.

Beneath the thin veneer of domestication, this animal is wild at heart, with an independence of spirit that can never really be tamed. Unlike the totally dependent dog, cats can fend for themselves if they have to. Indeed, millions of alley cats do not know any other way of life.

Communication

Cats recognize each other initially by smell. Friendly cats greet one another by touching noses or rubbing their foreheads together. They may rub their bodies together and sniff at each other's genital regions.

The alert cat has a direct gaze and points its ears and whiskers forwards. If it is also slightly nervous it will twitch its nostrils, attempting to identify by scent. When a person has been identified as a friend, the cat's expression relaxes, and its tail rises in greeting.

A cat under threat first freezes, staring at the aggressor with wide eyes. Its tail flicks slowly from side to side. If further threatened, the cat pulls in its chin, lays back its ears and gradually runs sideways on to the enemy. Simultaneously the hairs on the body and tail begin to become erect, presenting the largest possible body area. The cat draws back its lips to reveal its teeth and growls an unmistakable warning. Its muscles are poised for either fight or flight, the weight of the body taken on three legs while the fourth is held ready to strike.

Feline body-language

Cats are masters in the art of body-language, conveying their moods and intentions by a series of well-defined postures, clearly understood by humans, as well as fellow felines.

Cats use a variety of sounds in communicating with humans. This cat is voicing feelings of nervousness.

This Blue Smoke Persian is obviously upset and emitting an extremely loud yowl.

An unhappy, lilac Burmese squats into a defensive posture with wide eyes and flattened ears.

An agitated, nervous cat is dangerous to touch, for it may react as violently as if receiving an electric shock. Such a cat will be crouched down with tucked-in chin, wide eyes and ears held sideways. It must be talked out of this state and calmed down, or left in peace and quiet to recover its composure.

Experts are not sure where cats produce the sound of purring. Some think it is the sound of turbulence in the main vein of the heart. Others suspect that when cats arch their backs the blood vibrates throughout their bodies, creating sounds that resonate in the sinuses. Most experts, however, think purring is produced by vibrations of membranes, called false vocal cords, located close to the vocal cords.

Most cats can make a range of sounds in three basic categories. The quietest is similar to a human murmur and includes soft purring. Murmurs are made with the mouth closed. The middle category of feline sounds may be thought of as vowel sounds, each being a variation of the 'miaow', and each being used to express a different need, such as asking to be let out.

The most interesting range of cat talk is that made by a mother cat teaching her kittens to eat solid food, to

The typical tail-up greeting of a cat indicating its pleasure and soliciting a stroke from its owner.

follow her from the nest, and to behave properly. The kittens themselves are able to purr, spit and growl, and also have a loud distress call with which they cry to their mother when they are lost or frightened.

An American Wirehair rolls over to solicit attention.

The expressive body

The cat's body is almost as expressive as its face as a means of communication, and few parts of the body are more explicit than the tail.

By elevating the tail and bristling the fur, the cat can give most prospective enemies good reason to have second thoughts. No matter how confident the foe, it must be intimidating to find that a one foot high pushover is suddenly transformed into a menace almost two feet tall.

A dog can do the same thing in a smaller way by raising the hackles on its back, and even the tiny hamster can make itself look frighteningly larger by puffing out its cheeks. However, the cat is in a class of its own.

In addition to the hair on the tail, it can, of course, raise all the hair on its body. It is not clear how much control the cat has over this action, but it certainly has an unnerving effect on the average canine interloper. Tail language is not limited to threat. The same fluffed-up appearance can indicate fear. In this event, the tail is more likely to be held close to the ground.

During ambush and just before the pounce – whether in play or real hunting – the tail is rigid, with the tip gently gyrating. Some would say that it is like an engine warming up for take-off. The angry cat will also clearly indicate displeasure by swishing its tail from side to side. The abject cat may pull its tail between its legs, rather like a dog.

Cats will also use their limbs to communicate. A paw may be extended in friendship, cupboard love, or in a manner indicating danger. Whether in defence or offence, a paw with the claws out is something which must be treated with respect. A gentle pat with a clawless paw is usually a means of letting you know that the cat is ready for a game, or a stroke. Many an owner has been woken up with the gentle, but unnerving, pat on the face.

The hind limbs obviously are not so communicative. Although they cannot match the rabbit's hind legs as weapons, an adversary can be certain that the cat is in deadly earnest when it brings them into battle.

The way in which a cat walks has a myriad of meanings, most of them quite obvious. For example, the cat which bounds about with all four legs stiffly outstretched is ready for an

Left A gentle pat with a clawless paw is usually a means of letting you know that the cat is ready for a game, or a stroke. Many an owner has been woken up with the gentle, but unnerving, pat on the face.

Left *The angry cat will also clearly indicate displeasure by swishing its tail from side to side.*

energetic game. However, the feline which walks away from a companion, animal or human, in a stiff-legged, deliberately slow fashion, is probably saying, 'You are so far beneath me that you are not worthy of notice at all.'

If this haughty attitude provokes a hostile reaction, the cat will simply become even more infuriating. It will run out of reach and start to groom itself, which clearly says, 'I don't know what the fuss is about. As you can see, I am very busy with my own affairs.'

Everyone has a way of interpreting their cat's behaviour. All cats are different, and we see them all differently. Who is to say how they see us?

Right *The classic 'tail up' greeting that all owners are familiar with especially at meal times.*

THE FAMILY FOCUS

Cats will sit for hours in front of the television set, but how much they see, appreciate or enjoy is highly debatable. The same cat will continue to sit in the same position even if the set is switched off, provided its adopted human family are sitting in their customary positions.

Cats definitely can see the images on the television screen, for their eyesight is as good, if not better, than ours. Many learning experiments have shown that they can discriminate between shapes. For example, if they are shown crosses and circles, with one combination representing a reward of food, and another representing shock, they will quickly learn which to choose.

In the same way, cats can discriminate between colours, but probably not to the same degree as humans. There is no way in which a cat's mind can translate the constantly changing shapes it sees on the screen into any sort of meaningful action.

The hearing of cats is possibly more acute than ours. They can hear beyond the human range and into the higher frequencies. This is probably the reason why cats respond more readily to a woman's voice. Incidentally, it is also thought that this sensitivity to higher frequencies enables the cat to hear the voices of rodents as it waits hopefully by the mousehole.

Cats will, of course, prick up their ears in reaction to violent movement on a screen, or to an ear-splitting shriek, or the piteous cries of a baby. Anything that resembles the sights and sounds of their own lives may evoke a reaction. However, by and large, cats nod off in front of the television, and who is to blame them?

As any owner knows, cats are great lovers of their creature comforts. Unerringly, they pick and occupy the best seats in the theatre of life. In many homes the television set is the focus of family relaxation and well-being.

The thoroughly domesticated cat finds much comfort in the company of its family. If that family consists of more than one person, there is almost always a particular individual to whom the cat will devote most attention.

This is particularly true of all queens and neutered toms, for in the normal situation, the whole tom might provide the essential feeling of security. In the human family it is usually the wife who provides the cat's basic necessities, and it is to her that the animal gives its allegiance. If she is watching TV, so will the cat; if she decides to run the sewing machine instead, the cat will desert the screen to watch the bobbing needle.

Some dogs will insist on accompanying discordant or high notes with a sympathetic howl. In fact, dogs can hardly restrain themselves from yawning when in the company of people who are obviously bored. Cats do not react in this way, because they lead an essentially solitary life. Neither social howling nor social yawning plays any part. Like its ancestors, the modern domesticated cat remains silent.

Sight and sound may vary in their effect on the cat, but no stimulus provokes more response than an interesting smell. Everyone knows that felines are greatly attracted to the plant known as catnip, or catmint, though no one is wholly sure why it should have this effect. The smell of food will instantly demand the attention of any self-respecting cat, which is alert to even the most oblique hint of a meal. Most cats dislike rain, but wet weather brings out worms, and therefore birds. For such pleasures, a cat may be prepared to tolerate a soaking.

Familiar faces

Where cats are concerned, familiarity breeds acceptance. As long as they stay together, cats which have been reared in each other's company will remain on reasonably polite terms. However, like other animals, a cat will react most unfavourably to another which has been absent from home.

The rat, by any standards an intelligent creature, is an excellent example of the extremes to which animals will go. They recognize fellow inhabitants of the home by their odour. Remove the rat from its own area for only an hour, so that its odour changes, and it will be torn to pieces by its neighbours on its return.

With cats, this process of defamiliarization takes several days. They do not go to the extreme of killing the unfortunate returning animal, but they will make its life difficult.

One Siamese breeding establishment reports that it brings its adult queens into the family home on a rota basis for varying periods. This is done because the kittens of animals which have little contact with family life tend to remain timid and suspicious of people.

The two champion queens, Bella and Tiger Lily, were sisters which had been reared together, and had their first litters together in a communal kennel. The kittens suckled both mothers without discrimination.

A few months later, Bella was transferred into the family home, with Tiger Lily following six weeks later. They acted as if they had never seen each other before, going through the whole ritual of hostility, claws out and hissing. Two weeks passed before they managed to establish a neutrality.

Conversely, anyone with knowledge of animal husbandry will confirm that it is not difficult to introduce

an orphan – even one of an unrelated species – to a nursing mother. The memory of unpleasant experiences lingers longer in a cat's mind. Most vets can tell tales of walking into a house which they have not visited for three or four years to be greeted by the sight of vanishing tails.

The mint mystery

Show a cat catnip, and it will show you a change in its behaviour and personality. Even a most reserved animal will shrug off its inhibitions – purring loudly, growling, rolling around and even going to the extreme of leaping into the air. Nepata cataria, a species of mint, has this unfailingly ecstatic effect on cats. Even lions are not immune. No one knows why catnip does this, but theorists have suggested that it is an aphrodisiac for cats.

also learn of the amount of inbreeding that has taken place in the cat's ancestors and the animal's relationship to other, possibly noted and prized, bloodlines.

A pedigree with gaps can be like a recipe with key ingredients not listed. The result of breeding the animal, or making the dessert, is anyone's guess. And, of course, just as in making a fine dessert, variables will enter into the process occasionally, giving us something that no one could have anticipated. Mutation is one of those variables in breeding. It is explained more fully under the section on selective breeding.

Exactly when a breed or variety gets its official 'papers' depends on the registering organization, of which there may be quite a few. Some allow kittens to be registered to ensure that there will be proper record-keeping for several years prior to being admitted to show. Others demand that several generations of the potential new breed first be produced. Still others insist that a certain number of cats or breeders be involved with a new breed before it can be recognized.

Maine Coon

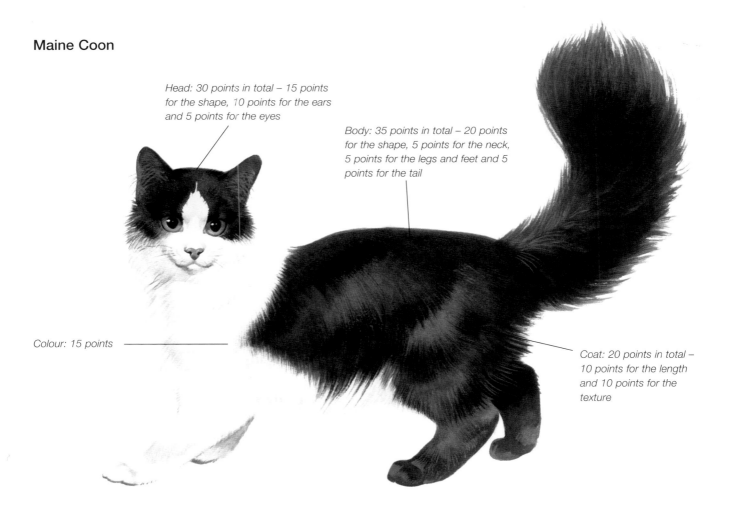

Head: 30 points in total – 15 points for the shape, 10 points for the ears and 5 points for the eyes

Body: 35 points in total – 20 points for the shape, 5 points for the neck, 5 points for the legs and feet and 5 points for the tail

Colour: 15 points

Coat: 20 points in total – 10 points for the length and 10 points for the texture

How many cat breeds are there?

For the first several thousand years of their association with man, cats were functional animals kept for their mousing abilities or were pets kept mainly for their companionship. But it was only a matter of time until the feline's great natural diversity gave rise to the concept of breeding.

In the mid-19th century in Europe, particularly in Great Britain, owners began to take pride in the specific characteristics of their animals and to attempt to breed them to refine and enhance those characteristics. Proud owners had exhibited their cats as early as the 16th century, but the first show that could really be called a show by modern standards was held in 1871 at the Crystal Palace in London. There were 25 show classes, divided into either Eastern or British.

Initially, the breeding efforts focused upon those cats that had become native to the British Isles. But travellers were soon bringing back exotic-looking cats, first the Persians and later the Siamese.

Associations sprang up to oversee and regulate the breeding and showing activity. Founded in Britain in 1887 The National Cat Club was the first. Others followed and came together in 1910 as The Governing Council of the Cat Fancy. In 1983 a breakaway group formed the Cat Association of Britain.

Several similar organizations have developed in the United States. The American Cat Association is the oldest, but the Cat Fanciers' Association is the largest. Others include the American Cat Fanciers' Association, Cat Fanciers' Federation, Crown Cat Fanciers' Federation, United Cat Federation and International Cat Association.

The Canadian Cat Association is the governing body for Canada, while the Fédération Internationale Féline de l'Europe is the largest in continental Europe.

Not all organizations recognize the same breeds. For example, only a few US organizations recognize the hairless Sphynx, and while the Scottish Fold is recognized in the United States, it is not officially recognized by the Governing Council in Britain.

Despite the differences, or maybe because of them in some instances, about 100 pedigree breeds are now recognized. That number reflects duplication in that some major organizations classify some breeds differently. All breeds generally fall into one of four categories: Longhairs, Siamese, Shorthairs and Foreign Shorthairs. However, that is far from an all-inclusive total.

Some breeds, such as the Snowshoe, are so new that breed standards have not been fully developed to allow for their official recognition. Others, such as the Sphynx and Scottish Fold, remain highly controversial, with some strong feelings against even continuing these lines.

Left *The Snowshoe is such a new breed that breed standards have not been fully developed to allow for their official recognition.*

Today, Persians are the most popular breed – if measured in sheer numbers of cats entered into shows – in the cat fancy, the term that covers the breeding and judging of pedigreed cats. The enthusiasts of most other breeds would naturally argue the point.

But the cat fancy encompasses only a small minority of the many millions of owners of cats; they may be the most vocal owners in favour of their own particular breed, but they are a minority nonetheless.

Much of the rest of our large fraternity of cat owners would be hard pressed to classify their cat or cats any further than feline. There's no need. Pedigree or moggie (the term for a non-pedigree cat), the cat that shares the house with you is without a doubt the best cat on the face of the Earth. In addition, many cat clubs provide for the showing of non-pedigree, well-cared for, and well-groomed house cats or crossbreeds that cannot be placed in a specific breed class.

Another consideration, of course, is the cost. Moggies are available for free at all times. Animal shelters have more than they can ever place; advertisements in newspapers constantly offer free cats to good homes.

Pedigrees, on the other hand, carry a price tag that generally reflects the fame and fortunes of the cat's bloodline, and the effort that has gone into building that line. While most of these prices are not all that

Above *The Persian is arguably the most popular breed entered into shows.*

high, some sought-after, champion-line kittens fetch prices that will turn a head or two. For some particularly unusual varieties there are even waiting lists of several years.

The 100 breeds that exist today should not be considered the final number of breeds. The past few decades have seen the creation of several new ones, and there are probably more to come.

Have any breeds disappeared?

Have you ever seen a Mexican Hairless? Not the nicknamed dog, but the specific breed of cat? Probably not. It is a lost breed, bred only briefly in the late 1800s in Mexico.

The Mexican Hairless is one lost breed that we know about. There have been others, lost because of lack of interest and for other reasons. But how many potential breeds have been lost without the cat fancy even knowing about them?

Although mutations are not commonplace, every day happenings, they do occur regularly enough for us to be certain that many more than have been made public have actually appeared in litters around the world. Perhaps owners failed to recognize the potential in the mutation, or even destroyed the 'different' animal. Perhaps pressure to destroy it was put on them by local cat owners. For whatever reasons, they kept the mutation to themselves and it was lost – at least for the time – with the death of an individual cat.

For example, a white variety of the Russian Blue was bred experimentally for a time in Great Britain. But, due to lack of widespread interest, much of the breeding programme has been dropped, and the variety is now quite rare.

Below This 17th-century Flemish painting depicts a strange, moustachioed cat with an unnervingly 'human' face.

The human whim has also brought some breeds that are widespread and popular today to near extinction. When the Persian was first gaining popularity among the cat fancy in Great Britain, it did so primarily at the expense of the closely related Turkish Angora. As a result, the Turkish Angora was slowly moving towards extinction.

However, more recent popularity in the United States has brought the Turkish Angora a new lease of life. The breed is in the midst of a major revival, freshened with new blood from cats imported from the Ankara Zoo in Turkey.

Conversely, popularity almost drove the Siamese into extinction. As the breed became fashionable in the 1920s, breeders were hard pressed to keep up with demand. As a result they took shortcuts, including repeated inbreeding, that nearly destroyed the bloodlines. In the nick of time, some breeders recognized the threat to the breed and reinstituted the careful breeding procedures needed to ensure the continuation of a strong, healthy breed.

The Abyssinian came similarly close to the brink of disappearance much more recently, albeit not because of its popularity. During World War I and World War II, food scarcities struck everywhere in the European community. Meat, the essential dietary item of the Abyssinian even more so than many other breed, was in short supply, even for human consumption.

The breed was nearly extinct at the close of World War II. It had made a recovery by the 1960–70s, but then it was devastated by mass outbreaks of the feline leukaemia virus. Although it is rather rare, the Abyssinian is an extremely popular cat and is now enjoying another strong period of recovery.

A look into the future of cat breeds is as simple as a visit to the section of any well-stocked pet shop that houses hamsters, guinea pigs and mice. There you'll find new coat types that mutation has yet to produce in cats or that man has yet to decide to encourage.

Perhaps the next breed of cat will have the rosette coat, with hair growing outwards in all directions from various starting points across the body. Or maybe the satin coat, with its light-reflecting hairs, will capture a group of supporters.

When you consider how far we have come in just over 100 years, from the first cat show at the Crystal Palace in 1871 with its 25 different judging classes, nothing seems impossible.

Left *The Abyssinian came close to the brink of disappearance at the end of World War II, but numbers had started to make a recovery by the 1960–70s.*

Selective breeding

From time to time anomalies occur in litters of kittens, in both pedigrees and domestics, and quite often, breeders fascinated by all things new or unusual may decide to try to perpetuate the unusual features and perhaps produce a new breed. It is possible, after selectively breeding one or several generations, to determine the genetic make-up of a new feline feature, and then to set out a formal and constructive breeding programme to develop a new breed. Some features which are clearly detrimental to a cat's well-being would be frowned upon by true cat lovers, and would thus prove unacceptable to most associations for registration and breeding purposes.

Scottish Fold
Refused recognition by some associations on the premise that the tightly folded ears are impossible to keep clean and healthy, and because some skeletal anomalies were apparent in some early Fold kittens.

American Curl
The curled ears of this breed do not appear to present any problems, and the breed is accepted by some associations in the United States of America.

Sphynx
Those who love the apparently hairless Sphynx work tirelessly for its recognition for show and registration. Others consider that a breed which may not be viable in the wild state should not be encouraged.

Breeding pedigree cats

Breeding pedigree cats is a hobby that should not be undertaken lightly. Only cats of the very best quality and with strong constitutions should be kept for breeding and they must be expertly and considerately cared for.

Although ordinary domestic cats seem to become pregnant and produce kittens without much bother, often against their owners' wishes, the production of pedigree kittens under controlled conditions, however, can prove difficult. Despite its many generations of domestication, a cat can resent the unnatural restrictions placed upon her during mating and pregnancy. She may prove unwilling to mate with the stud cat chosen for her; she may have a stressful gestation period or a difficult delivery. She could reject her kittens, have little or poor quality milk or be so unsettled as to spend her time anxiously moving the kittens to new nest sites.

A successful cat breeder will be someone for whom financial gain is not important. Breeding pedigree cats is a hobby full of rewards, but none of these is financial. There is a great sense of pride and achievement in planning a special litter, seeing it born and rearing it. A true cat lover will gain a great deal from caring for the female cat, known as the brood queen, helping her through the weeks of pregnancy, attending the birth, and looking after the needs of the growing family. On the debit side is the problem of parting with the kittens when they are fully independent and ready to go to new homes at about three months old.

It may seem logical to buy a pair of cats in order to start breeding, but this is impractical. Keeping a stud male is not a job for the novice. He will not be content with a monogamous relationship with one queen, and needs special accommodation of his own so that his habit of spray-marking his territory with strong-smelling urine does not become a serious household problem.

Starting out

To start breeding it is best to buy one or two females of the breed you have chosen, seeking advice from an experienced breeder or show judge, and purchasing the very best females that you can afford. Two females will keep each other company, and if they are unrelated you will have a good foundation for lines of your own in future years. A kitten for breeding should be purchased at about three months old. She should be of sound conformation, with a good temperament and an impeccable pedigree, and should be properly registered with an acceptable cat association. She should be well grown for her age and should have received a suitable course of vaccinations for which you will be provided with certificates. Until she grows to adulthood, the kitten should lead a normal life,

Left *Breeding pedigree cats is a hobby that should not be undertaken lightly. Only cats of the very best quality and with strong constitutions should be kept for breeding and they must be expertly and considerately cared for. A successful cat breeder will be someone for whom financial gain is not important. Breeding pedigree cats is a hobby full of rewards, but none of these is financial.*

short nose and large, round eyes. The other feature these cats have in common is an exceptionally full coat. It is called a double coat because it has both a soft, woolly undercoat and a slightly longer, coarser coat up to 11.5cm (4.5in) long. The longhaired cats that are not Persian come from cold climates where a long coat is useful. Their coats are not usually as woolly or as full as those of Persians. They are also slimmer, longer and easier to groom.

Short hair is far more common because the genes for short hair are dominant over those for long hair. Unlike long hair, a short coat is generally easy to care for: simpler to clean, it won't tangle, and is less likely to cause hairballs or blockages within the digestive system. It also has health advantages, as wounds can be more easily cared for and parasites can be caught earlier.

Whether your cat is Persian – the most popular breed in the cat fancy (the world of cat breeding and showing) – or something of less blue-blood ancestry, you can enjoy and compete in cat shows. To enter, contact the sponsoring organization for an entry form. You will also receive show rules, which are laid down to ensure fairness and protect the interests of the cat.

For example, usually after showing, you must wait at least a week before exhibiting again. Another rule usually prohibits the use of anything that could alter the cat's appearance. These rules vary between countries and even between different regions and organizations, so be sure to check.

The usual procedure is to enter your cat or kitten in one basic colour class for its breed according to its status, i.e. Open, Champion or Grand Champion. It will be judged in this class, as well as in every all-breed and speciality competition for which it is eligible. On show day, you'll need the following equipment and supplies: travelling container, litter pan, feeding dish, food, water bowl, water bottle, show blanket, grooming tools, favourite toy, vaccination certificates and other paperwork that the particular show requires.

Coat types in different breeds

A cat's coat may consist of three hair types:

 top coat or guard hairs

bristly awn hairs

undercoat or down hairs

Persian (Longhair) *Dense with long guard hairs of up to 12.5cm (5in) and thick down hairs.*

Angora *Finer than the Persian; both guard and down hairs are very long.*

Maine Coon *Down and guard hairs are long, like the Persian, but shaggy and uneven.*

Devon Rex *Guard, awn and down hairs all very curly and short.*

British Shorthair *Sparse awn hairs with guard hairs of about 4.5cm (2in).*

Sphynx *No guard or awn hairs; just a few down hairs on face, legs and tail.*

The first thing that happens on show day is called 'vetting-in' – a thorough health check by a veterinarian. If for some reason – fleas, soreness, running nose – the cat fails the examination, you will be disqualified and forfeit your entry fee. Make sure your cat is used to travelling by car; if it has symptoms of motion sickness, it may be disqualified.

After vetting-in, you can take your cat to its pen – a metal cage displaying the cat's show entry number. (Because your cat will need to be penned during much of the show, you should accustom it to being penned. Begin by penning it for a few minutes a day, and progressively lengthen the time.) Take some time to arrange the pen for comfort and eye appeal. Many owners put a lot of effort into assuring that the decoration highlights the cat's colouring. (In the UK, however, show equipment must be white in most competitions.)

Cats are taken to the judge's table one at a time. For this part of the judging, you should get your cat used to being held up at arm's length as a judge would when examining it. Place one hand under the front legs, and scoop it up by pushing your other band under its hind quarters. Bring the cat up level with your chest, supporting its full weight underneath and leaning the cat against you. A kitten is small enough to sit on your palm as long as you have your other hand around its neck to support the head.

For each pedigree breed there is a standard of points against which the cat is evaluated. For non-pedigree cats, there is no scale of points, so the cat is judged on condition, grooming, colouring, attractive features and temperament when handled.

Once the judge has examined every cat in a class, the judge personally places the rosettes on the pens in the winning order and the results are then announced. After the various judges have nominated their five best cats and five best neuters, a top judge assesses all these cats until the five best in each section have been chosen. Eventually, an overall 'Best Cat' is chosen.

Left Whether your cat is a pedigree like this Egyptian Mau, or something of less blue-blood ancestry like the moggie kitten below, everyone can enjoy and compete in cat shows.

FELINE ASSOCIATIONS

Countries where pedigree cats are bred and exhibited have one or more associations or governing bodies which keep a register of cats and their lineage, and set down rules and regulations for cat shows. Britain has the Governing Council of the Cat Fancy (GCCF) and The Cat Association of Britain, which is the British member of FIFe. American cat fanciers have nine associations, the largest being the Cat Fancier's Association (CFA) which also has affiliated clubs in Canada and Japan.

In Europe, Australasia and South Africa, there are national bodies, and other associations, and, generally, one in each country is a member of the Federation Internationale Feline (FIFe) which is the largest and most powerful of the feline associations in the world. FIFe has thousands of members, covering the entire world of cats and trains and licenses judges of high calibre throughout the world.

CANADA

CCA The Canadian Cat Association is the only all-Canadian registry, with activities centred mainly in eastern Canada. It publishes a bilingual, quarterly newsletter in French and English.

UNITED STATES

ACA The oldest cat registry, active since 1899, the American Cat Association is a fairly small association which holds shows in the south-east and south-west of the United States.

ACC Based in the south-west, the American Cat Council is a small association which has modified 'English-style' shows in which exhibitors must vacate the show hall during judging.

CCFF Although one of the smaller associations, the Crown Cat Fanciers' Federation has many shows each year in the north-east and south-east, and also in western Canada.

CFA The Cat Fanciers' Association is America's largest association, incorporated and run by a board of directors. It produces an impressive annual yearbook full of articles, breeders' advertisements and beautiful colour photographs. There is a CFA show somewhere in the United States almost every weekend of the year.

CFF With activities centred in the north-east region of the United States, the Cat Fanciers' Federation is a registering body of medium size.

UCF A medium-sized association, the United Cat Federation is centred in the south-west of the United States.

UNITED KINGDOM

CA Formed on 20th February 1983 as an alternative body to the GCCF, the Cat Association of Britain keeps a register of all pedigree, half-pedigree and non-pedigree cats belonging to its members, and holds cat shows all over Britain. Formerly run as an independent association, CA became a member of FIFe (right) in 1991.

GCCF Formed on 8th March 1910, the Governing Council of the Cat Fancy is run by an executive committee, and its 60 or so affiliated clubs send delegates to represent their members at council meetings. Until 1983, GCCF was the sole body responsible for the registration of cats and licensing of cat shows in Britain.

WORLDWIDE

ACFA An international association and run very democratically, the American Cat Fanciers' Association has affiliated clubs in the United States, Canada and Japan, and produces a monthly news bulletin for members.

FIFe Most European countries have at least two bodies for the registration of cats, and licensing of shows. One body is almost certain to be affiliated to the Fédération Internationale Feline, a well-organized incorporated and chartered society which also has affiliates in countries beyond Europe. Established in 1949, FIFe is today the largest cat body in the world uniting more than 150,000 breeders and exhibitors.

TICA The International Cat Association produces a bi-monthly newsletter and a yearbook. It has a modern approach and has shows throughout the USA and affiliates in Canada and Japan.

THE FELINE GOURMET

Early man used to throw left-over food and bones at animals lurking outside his cave. His intention was to discourage them, but it merely convinced certain animals that man could simplify the eternal quest for food, by handing it to them, almost on a plate.

The cat was among those animals and since then it has moved right into the home. However, its approach remains unchanged. When meat is being prepared, children are eating cereal or a cow is being milked … the cat is there.

Cat-lovers will recognize the obvious ploys, such as piteous mewing or dog-like begging.

Even in rich, urbanized societies, where most pets are overfed, cats persist in begging. One explanation is that the cat becomes addicted to eating, just as some people are hooked on nicotine or alcohol.

How much should a cat eat? A simple rule is 25g (1oz) of food per 25g (1oz) of body weight while growing, and half that amount for the adult. Like humans, cats vary considerably in their ability to utilize food, and in their daily expenditure of energy.

If your cat is overweight, take it to the vet to make sure there is no underlying physical cause. If the obesity is because of overfeeding, cut the food intake by five or ten per cent, until it is down by 50 per cent.

Because cats are covered with hair, it is sometimes difficult to judge weight. Also, owners tend not to notice gradual changes. If the adult cat gains only 100g (4oz) a year, by the time it reaches an age of 10 or 11 it may be a quarter to a third overweight.

The cat's traditional diet is the small rodent. The mouse is a real meal, providing 70 per cent water, 14 per cent protein, 10 per cent fat, one per cent carbohydrate and one per cent mineral. The liver is full of vitamins and the bones contain calcium. The ideal manufactured cat food should approximate to that formula.

Apparently normal cats, eating the recommended diet, will still dash straight from the bowl into the garden and eat the grass. This behaviour is not confined to the domestic cat. Lions in game reserves can be seen in the mornings grazing like cattle. Although no one knows for sure why they do it, one can only assume that fresh grass contains nutrients lacking in the regular diet.

Cats also eat grass in an attempt to soothe inflammation of the throat, or when they have an irritation in the bowel. This type of grass-eating is characterized by a compulsive, almost frantic, urge, the cat seeking out coarse, dry shoots. If the unfortunate animal has swallowed a noxious substance, or has accumulated some hairballs, this is an effective way of inducing vomiting and helping to relieve the discomfort or distress.

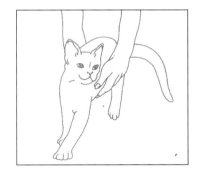

The rib test

The rib test remains a reasonably effective guide to whether or not a cat's weight is correct. If you cannot feel each rib individually, without exerting undue pressure, then the cat is probably too fat. If the ridges of the cat's ribs feel like pencils, the chances are that it is not being fed enough, or that it is suffering from a condition which needs immediate attention from your vet.

Feeding Your Cat

An adult cat requires about 50 calories per 450 g (1 lb) of its body weight each day. Active cats may need more calories and sedentary cats may need less. Entire cats which are breeding require more calories than neutered cats, and a queen that is lactating, and feeding four or more kittens, may need as much as 150 calories for each 450 g (1 lb) of her body weight.

Adult cats generally fare better when given two regular daily meals, and as they grow old, they are best fed three or four small meals daily. Old cats with digestive problems often need special diets as advised by a veterinary surgeon.

A cat's general appearance is the best guide to whether or not its diet is suitable for its size and lifestyle.

The signs of a poor diet include dull eyes, a warm, dry nose, bad breath, a dry scurfy coat, flaking claws and diarrhoea or offensively smelling stools.

There are a number of excellent ways of feeding cats. Canned food is comparatively expensive, but it is formulated to be highly acceptable to cats, and a check on the label will ensure that the quality and nutritional components are adequate.

Semi-moist diets are very convenient to store and serve, and are highly acceptable to most cats. However, they contain humectants and preservatives which can cause digestive disturbances in some cats. Owners often get round this problem by feeding one meal of canned food and one of semi-moist food each day.

Dry diets are very popular, particularly for pet cats.

What to feed

This chart shows you at a glance how many feeds to give your cat on a daily basis.

Cat details		Food requirements	
age of cat	cat weight (g)	feeds	gms per feed
Kitten			
Newborn	110	10	30
5 weeks	450	6	85
10 weeks	900	5	140
20 weeks	2,000	4	170
30 weeks	3,000	3	200
Adult			
Male/Female	3,000–4,500	1-2	170–240
Pregnant	3,500	2-3	240
Lactating	2,500	4	400
Neuter	4,000–4,500	1-2	170–200

They are inexpensive, and very easy to store and serve. It is important to ensure that cats fed solely on dry diets are seen to drink plenty of water every day. Some brands may be slightly deficient in fat, so extra fat may be given if necessary.

Energy requirements
An adult cat needs 200 to 300kcal per day, depending on its size and amount of exercise. Kittens have a higher demand in relation to their body weight due to their rapid growth rate. Neutered cats need less energy in relation to their body weight as they are not reproducing and generally lead rather sedentary lives.

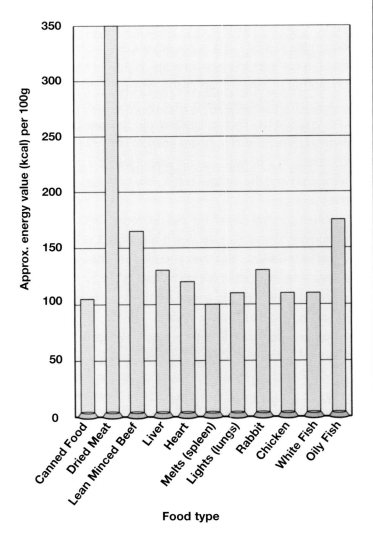

Food type

Nutritional requirements

Proteins essential substances for growth and repair; they are found in muscle meat, fish, cheese, eggs and milk. At least 35–40 per cent of the entire cat's diet should consist of protein; neutered cats need 25 per cent. Cats which cannot digest milk or milk products may be able to accept yoghurt as an alternative.

Carbohydrates not essential in the cat's diet, and if fed, should consist of cooked grains and vegetable fibre.

Fats provide concentrated forms of energy, and the cat is capable of digesting a diet containing 25 to 30 per cent fat. Fats contain the fatty acids necessary for a healthy skin and coat, and fat-soluble vitamins A, D, E and K. Fats may be added to the cat's diet in the form of butter, margarine, bacon fat or pure vegetable oils.

Vitamins and minerals found in a wide range of foods. Cats need a lot of Vitamin A, but too much can be dangerous. If using a proprietary brand of cat food, check the label for the Vitamin A level. If feeding fresh meat, add 28g (1oz) of lightly cooked liver on one or two days each week.

Vitamin B is important to cats, and you should check the labels of proprietary brands of food to ensure that the B group content is adequate.

Vitamin C is generally considered to be unnecessary in the feline diet, though it may help recovery after illness. Most cats accept Vitamin C in the form of an orange-flavoured syrup sold for human babies.

Vitamin D is essential, but cats need a very small amount compared to the requirements of dogs and humans, and most of this need is obtained from sunlight. It is rarely necessary to supplement the diet with additional vitamins and minerals provided an adequate diet is fed.

Lifting and carrying

A cat must be held safely and securely and never hurt during the process. If possible, handle it so that it does not hurt you either, which is sometimes easier said than done.

Kittens may be held and carried exactly as its mother does it. Grip the scruff of the neck and get on with it. The kitten will not mind, for its neck area is strong and its body weight light. As it puts on weight, this method will cause pain, and the growing cat will react accordingly.

The grip on the neck remains a good way of initially securing the animal, supporting the body with a firm, but gentle grasp of abdomen or hindquarters. If you are moving a kitten a fair distance, snuggle it next to you, while retaining a grip on the neck. Point its face and front legs away from you. If held securely against your body, the kitten should feel safe enough to relax. Although most children have little knowledge of how to handle a cat, they seem able instantly to communicate their feelings to the animal. Often, even the most disagreeable feline will respond by leaping into the child's arms and cuddling into the most comfortable position, purring all the while. The cat may even join in a game in which it is dressed in an assortment of bonnets and socks, or even wrapped in bandages borrowed from the first aid box.

Some cats are almost impossible to handle by the scruff of the neck. The most obvious are full toms in peak physical condition. They have no loose skin to speak of, and their necks and shoulders are muscled like a Bull Terrier. Few men have enough strength in their fingers to hold an unwilling tom in one hand.

Contrary to popular belief, many of these powerful cats are among the gentlest of creatures, if they are not riled. Try a little soothing conversation with the animal before going any further.

In common with many elderly cats, some younger ones suffer from arthritis of the spine and neck and simply cannot bear pressure on these joints. The neck area is a typical site of heavy flea-bite infection, or abscesses. One can hardly blame the cat if it responds adversely to squeezing of a painful area. The sensible solution is to look before you reach.

How does one hold and carry a cat without applying neck pressure? A gentle cat, that knows and trusts you, will often allow you to scoop it up with a hand under its chest and the other around its hindquarters or abdomen. Others may have to be picked up with one hand gripping the forelegs and the other the abdomen – the method used by judges during competitions at shows.

Correct and comfortable
The correct method of carrying your cat is with the face and front legs away from your body.

Top *The show judge's method is to grip the forelegs and hindquarters or abdomen.*

Below left *Even the most disagreeable of felines will allow itself to be cradled in a child's arms.*

Below right *A kitten can safely be held by the scruff of its neck alone, for its neck is strong, and its body weight relatively light.*

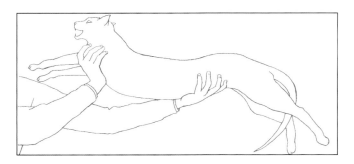

HOLDING OPERATION

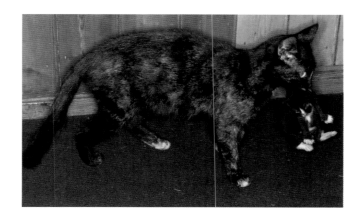

Many animals are on the move almost from birth, and the new-born antelope, for example, can outrun a fully grown wolf.

By contrast, the kitten is a helpless creature, totally reliant on its mother which is, in turn, reliant on the security of the nest she has built. If that security is threatened, she must move the kittens.

There is only one efficient way of doing this, and it is to grab them around the neck. The tail would not afford a hold, and neither would a limb. In either case, the kitten would bounce around and risk serious injury.

The neck and shoulder area has the great advantage of being near to the kitten's centre of gravity. The hunting cat carries its prey in exactly the same way, for the same reasons. Those of us who have had to carry a cat have discovered that they are less able to respond with a violent argument if their neck and shoulders are under strict control.

The mother may feel obliged to move for many reasons. A cat out in the wild may have to cope with such things as combine harvesters, which can flatten a thousand acres before breakfast. Few rural nests can be considered inviolate. Unless the nursing queen responds immediately to the sound of advancing machinery, the result is death.

In the domestic situation, the movement of kittens is seldom so pressing. The main reason for the switch may be neurosis, brought about by well-meaning, but unwelcome, members of the human family.

***Right** The domestic cat may feel obliged to move her litter for many reasons, although the most likely is human interference. She will then find a new nest and move the kittens one by one. Carrying them by the neck is not instinctive. It is, however, the most convenient method and mother soon learns what is best.*

Yet another reason may be cleanliness. As the kittens grow in size, so does the mess they make, and the fastidious queen may not be able to cope, so she moves house.

Unless the mother has had her kittens by the back door, she must make a move when the youngsters begin to explore. The kittens will need more space than the warm cupboard will allow to exercise their growing physical strength, and by then the mother will want to show them off to you.

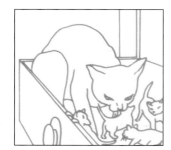

PLAY OR PRACTICE?

Play is basically a preparation for the realities of life, but how can we tell when an animal is playing? First, it does not seem to have any purpose and, second, the animal expends just that bit more energy than is really necessary. Simply, play is almost always characterized by exuberance, if not joy.

Watch closely and you will note that your cat will stop playing the moment a real problem or need arises. The kitten chasing a ball will suddenly forget all about it in order to deal with a flea. A litter of kittens engaged in mock combat will break off in mid-sprawl if they hear the clink of dinner bowls. However, a kitten taking part in a serious activity, like eating or stalking prey, will not allow play to intrude.

Right *Colourpoints are one of the more playful and inquisitive breeds.*

Some play has an obvious purpose or lesson. The cat playing with a toy mouse is preparing to deal with the real thing. Kittens which play-fight with each other or their mother are learning the art of feline defence and offence. Many an orphan reared by humans, without the company of a litter, has grown up into a timid and bewildered adult.

What of the many play activities for which there appears to be no reason? Dark, enclosed spaces hold an endless fascination. Tubes, tunnels, chimneys, washing machines, fridges, boxes or bags are just irresistible.

Some students of animal behaviour make the Freudian suggestion that it is simply a way of returning to the security of the nest. Some say they merely want a quiet place to sleep.

A rather far-fetched theory says that contact with the sides of the box or bag gratifies the cat's basically sensual nature. The same suggestion is made to explain why a cat will wind itself up in a ball of wool.

More likely, the cat finds in the many twisted strands endless objects to chase and countless enemies to vanquish.

Just for fun

One wonders how different the tests of animal behaviour would be if the academics who dominate the field were not the efficient and single-minded Germans and Americans. It is a safe bet that if the Italians were masters of this art, words like joy, pleasure, love, vitality and adventure would appear far more frequently.

It might even be accepted that many activities have absolutely no measurable purpose in terms of survival. You may think about it as long and hard as you like, and then feed your conclusions into a computer, but it is doubtful whether any scientific reason will be forthcoming as to why your cat enjoys playing with your typewriter.

An uncommonly high proportion of artistic people, such as painters, sculptors, writers, musicians or actors are cat devotees. This fascination certainly cannot be attributed to either stupidity or boredom. Perhaps it should be accepted that 'artistic sensibilities perceive motivations of cat behaviour that the more prosaic scientist has not yet managed to measure'.

However, even scientists will admit that some creatures, such as otters, dolphins and several crows, play for no other reason than pleasure.

The mother cat encourages play, and she supervises every minute of it. The kittens observe her carefully, and learn her signals and attitudes. Expressions of threat are 'taught' by the mother, and then the kittens try them out on her. The importance of this interplay is not as vital as it may seem, for orphaned kittens, reared alone, do not seem to have any difficulty in mastering the art of being threatening.

The most common forms of play are those which resemble fighting, escaping and hunting, but the distinction between fun and reality is striking.

A simple comparison will illustrate this point. A pack of hounds leaps the fence and goes for the cat. The terrified animal literally has to run for its life, and it will not stop until it is well and truly out of danger.

If, instead of the hounds, a friendly neighbourhood dog had jumped over the fence, the chase would have been a game greatly enjoyed by both participants. In fact, after a few yards, the escapee would turn and chase the attacker. Throughout the game, claws would remain sheathed and the teeth would not be bared.

Another major difference between the two situations is that the cat which is merely playing a game will instantly change from one posture to another. However, if it has recently escaped from real danger or threat to life, it will remain fully vibrant for several minutes.

In other words, a genuine activity has a clearly defined beginning and end. As it is when children play tag with each other, the game can start and end in the middle.

When survival is a genuine consideration, energy is conserved; in play there are no such limits.

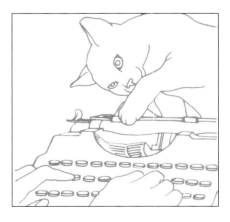

Left *Cats are ready to join in anything that their favourite human is doing. This may be merely watching the television, working at the sewing machine, playing the piano, or using a typewriter. Cats do not mind, for they are only too happy to 'help', whatever is going on.*

Cats are natural hunters. They are typical carnivores with jaws and teeth intended for eating flesh. Most domestic cats prefer to be lonely hunters, although it is not uncommon for them to hunt in pairs or even in groups. Kittens and cats play together, and play is a safe way of learning to hunt. It is observed that a mother cat will bring her young an injured bird or rodent, even though the kitten has no need of food. The reason appears obvious: she is teaching the kitten to pounce and kill. Later, when the offspring is more advanced, she will introduce the refinements of reconnaissance, ambush and the slink-run. The cat relies on stealth and surprise in hunting its prey and, although this killer instinct is regarded as one of its least attractive qualities, cats can be thanked for keeping down the vermin which would otherwise cause far more problems in society. Contrary to popular belief, cats are not great bird-catchers and usually have to make do with the lame and the hurt. In this way they are assisting the natural selection of nature.

Sabre-rattling

Animal aggression is a ritual, applying to cats as much as other species. The real name of this game is intimidation.

Take as an example creatures with antlers. They establish pecking order by butting each other, and they always meet head on. However frightening it looks, or how heavy the blows, it all forms part of a ritual designed to save the species from wiping itself out. Their skulls may ache, but both animals can walk away from battle. If the aggression was more than ritual, the stronger would have gone for the flank. If the area between ribs and hind leg was penetrated, it would mean certain death.

Cats behave in the same way. Feline signs of aggression are obvious; the hiss, and the well-displayed fangs; the pinpoint pupils; the ears pricked forward and every hair on the body raised.

Feline aggression is not a pretty sight; claws out, spitting, the teeth bared. The real warning sign is the backwards flattening of the ears. Only when they actually go on the attack do the ears flick forward. Deaf cats are among the few that do not issue a warning.

Public Enemy Number One

Everyone knows the old saying, 'They fight like cat and dog'. The dog is, of course, the cat's traditional and time-honoured Public Enemy Number One, but why should this be so? The main reason why cats are involved in more confrontations with dogs than any other alien species is simply that there are more of them about. Cats are willing to share their homes with dogs, but they are not all fond of canine outsiders.

Generally, cats are not afraid of other animals smaller than themselves. They are relegated to the status of potential meals, or just amusement. Creatures of equal or larger size are potential enemies and are treated as such until proved to be otherwise.

However, the cat certainly does not look upon even the tiniest of miniature dogs as a snack, and the powerful Great Dane would never consider eating a cat.

Obviously, the reasons for their inevitable hostility come down to such important animal matters as security, status and territory.

Many cats fancy their chances in a clash with a dog, and it is easy to see why. Most domesticated dogs are

Below *Even a tiny kitten, faced with an unknown canine, will put up a display of aggression that will warn off even a large dog.*

not really equipped to deal with the sheer ferocity and aggression of a hissing, spitting ball of fur, with sharp teeth and claws.

This would, of course, depend on the type of dog involved and, if there is more than one canine opponent, the ever-sensible cat will quickly opt for discretion rather than valour.

Most dogs in packs, particularly hounds, are potentially lethal, and not only to cats. These anti-social creatures are just as dangerous to other dogs, and even children who get in their way.

Almost as dangerous is any group of Greyhounds in training. They too will attack not only cats, but other dogs. Irate owners of savaged pets have made many demands for these racing animals to be muzzled while they are out on the streets.

Alsatians, Beagles and most Terriers and Corgis are other canine types which the cat should try to avoid.

Oddly enough, the formidable-looking Bulldog is a push-over for the average cat. However, at the bottom of the list of potential threats is the Pug, which could hardly be less pugnacious. Its ferocity is entirely vocal, and it will be treated by the cat with disdain and a tail in the air. Because of its size, the Pug runs the risk of serious eye injury if it foolishly chooses to stand and fight.

The cat living on the farm, or in the country, has three enemies which should be approached only if an escape has been planned in advance. These are weaning sows, confined dairy bulls and, most dangerous of all, cornered rats.

BEWARE OF THE CAT

Cats have been on the earth for about 50 million years, but they have been domesticated for only 3,000 of them. Therefore, it is not surprising if they have not yet quite accepted humans as their equals.

The alley cats which abound in the cities do not take to human handling at all. Some are difficult, but most are downright dangerous. If they were not, they would hardly be able to survive.

Many well-intentioned people have learned this the hard way. They rescue a kitten or litter, which has become separated from the mother, but no matter how patient or kind the humans are, these cats will rarely respond in anything other than a hostile fashion. The basic character seldom changes. If they come from wild, or semi-wild, stock that is the way they will remain.

Such cats are capable of a limited relationship with a human benefactor. In many cities, kind-hearted people will nightly feed the neighbourhood roamers. The animals will gather at the same spot, and will eat the food provided, but that is as far as it goes.

There will be no leg-rubbing, no stroking and certainly no miaow of gratitude. If the human ever tried to pick one up, the reward would be a clawed hand.

Surely household cats can be equally dangerous if provoked? They certainly can and, indeed, the only difference between them and their wild cousins is the threshold of tolerance. For example, the tom anxious to get out to find a queen on heat is not likely to be restrained by a human hand.

Cats of whatever sex, whether neutered or otherwise, which have been kept exclusively by a human female, will react unfavourably to handling by a man, and vice versa.

The best way to avoid this situation is clearly to allow kittens as wide a social circle as possible. The more people who handle the kittens during their vital formative months, the better.

Left *However well-bred or mannered our feline friends appear to be, below the surface of even the most tolerant cat is the flash of the wild cousin that roam our streets and cities.*

Territorial imperative

Like most humans, cats regard their home as their castle. This attitude towards territory extends beyond the confines of bricks and mortar. In built-up areas, a cat will regard an area of about one third of a mile as its own; in rural surroundings, a spread of about three miles is not at all unusual. This territoriality is a direct result of years of evolution to be solitary hunters.

These distances also depend on sex and the type of cat involved. A female neutered before her first season will feel secure only within the confines of her human family, but she may try to establish territorial rights within a short radius of the home.

On the other hand, the confident and aggressive tom will have a much broader and more ambitious outlook. In all cases, the boundaries of the territory are firmly fixed. Within them, a stranger runs the risk of attack; on the other side of the invisible lines, it will be left alone.

Cats work hard to avoid chance encounters with other cats, encounters which often lead to fighting and subsequent injury. As solitary predators, they rely entirely on their own ability to catch prey, so if their hunting skills are impaired, they are unable to survive.

In the wild, a cat establishes an area where it sleeps and eats its 'home base' and where it hunts and mates its 'home range'. The cat's territory radiates from roughly the centre of its home base and the size will generally relate to the availability of food. If food is plentiful, it deos not need a large home range, but if food is scarce, it does. The cat's territory consists of a network of paths that are patrolled regularly on a fairly fixed schedule. Cats mark their territory in four ways – scratching (leaving visual as well as scent marks), spraying, urine, or faeces deposits; and rubbing. These marks provide other cats with information about the individual cat (such as sex, age and health), as well as letting them know when the said cat was last there.

A typical territorial region around the suburban home.

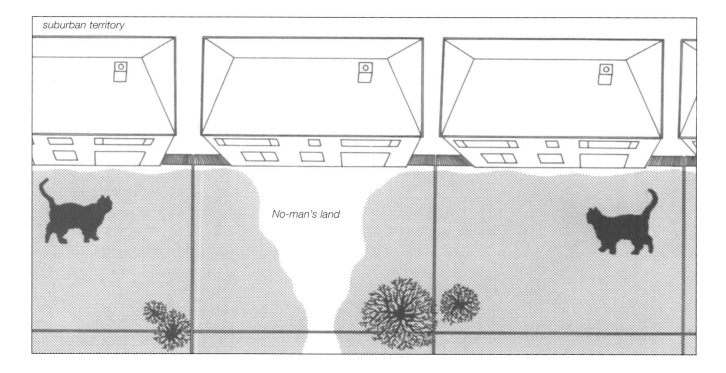

suburban territory

No-man's land

MATING AND REPRODUCTION

The female cat or queen makes a model mother, secreting her litter away from harm within a nest area. She feeds the kittens at regular intervals, keeps them spotlessly clean, and curls around them, purring, to rest and sleep. She will devote herself to their every need for as long as she needs to.

Mating

To become pregnant, your queen needs to be in oestrus (heat). Just before that period, she will be unusually affectionate and involve herself in more rubbing, rolling and licking than usual. When she enters oestrus, she will exhibit restlessness and anxiety to seek out a mate, howling and calling.

Feline heat cycles are seasonal in most breeds and tend to start in December or January until the following September. Most kittens arrive in July and August. Oestrus normally lasts about three weeks, but is only very noticeable for one week. When it begins, arrange for the queen and stud to spend time together. Relevant pedigree and health certificates should accompany the cats, and health checks may be required before the meeting begins. The two should be placed in adjacent quarters, separated by a door or mesh. When the queen begins to make advances, she should be allowed into his quarters. Either before or after mating, the queen may strike out at the tom, scratching, clawing and spitting. To protect himself, the male must have ample space to retreat during these periods.

Ejaculation occurs as soon as the tom enters the queen. Then they separate, and the tom distances himself from her. They should be permitted to mate several times over three or four days. It is most important to keep the queen in for a week after she has been to stud as she may still be calling and be mated by local tom cats. Dual conceptions are then possible; kittens born from dual conceptions cannot be registered with the GCCF.

The queen may not show signs of being pregnant until approximately two weeks after mating. If she is pregnant, her nipples will redden (pink-up), she will gain 1–2 kg (2–4 lb), her abdomen will swell, and she will become restless.

Pregnancy itself lasts about nine weeks (65 days). Kittens born earlier than 58 days tend to be delivered dead or weak and should be regarded as miscarriages. Those born later than 71 days are likely to be bigger than normal, and may be dead. Most queens have no trouble giving birth, but it's a good idea to keep the cat under veterinary care in case problems arise. Also make sure your queen eats a nutritious diet during her pregnancy, up to three or four meals a day if she desires.

Cats are exceptionally healthy creatures. In fact, the goat is the only domesticated animal which can compare. Very few queens abort or miscarry, and the vast majority will sail through pregnancy with no difficulty at all.

Mating

When a female cat is ready to mate, she adopts a characteristic hollowed back position, crouching and presenting her hindquarters, with her tail bent to one side. The male approaches her from the side and rear, running forward and grasping her by the loose skin at the scruff of the neck. He mounts her by straddling her body with his front legs, then arches his back in order to correctly position his penis for mating. The female also manoeuvres her pelvis to help penetration. After a few pelvic thrusts the male achieves penetration and quickly ejaculates. The female immediately pulls forward, growling fiercely, and attempts to turn and attack the male, who leaps away to safety. The female rolls, sometimes still growling, then both cats sit apart from each other and lick their own genital areas clean. After a few minutes, they will probably mate again.

Mating can occur up to ten times in an hour, or until the male is exhausted. If there are several males present, the female will mate with one or more of them in succession.

1 The male approaches from the side and rear.

2 He mounts by straddling the queen's body and grasping the loose skin at her scruff.

3 The queen assists mating by raising her pelvis and turning her tail to one side.

4 After mating the male leaps away and the female turns, spits and fiercely growls.

Although cats usually make it their business to land on their feet, any sort of fall during pregnancy can have bad effects, causing the animal to miscarry. An attack of flu or enteritis can do the same. If the miscarriage occurs in the early stages of pregnancy, the cat may show little signs of discomfort. As with humans, a miscarriage in the later stages is a more serious matter and will certainly require a visit from your vet. Some cats mate successfully and then come into heat again a few weeks later. In this event, you should either find her another tom, or find out if she is losing her kittens when they are very young. In some cases, a regime of enforced rest and a series of hormone injections are all that is needed to put the animal on the road to normal motherhood.

However, if this happens to a highly-valued, inbred queen, it is likely that the inbreeding has caused some internal abnormality. Such a queen should be spayed. Many confined feline females astonish their owners by swelling up, making milk, or cuddling up to objects as if they were kittens. These cats may also become morose, neurotic and aggressive and refuse their food. The owners simply cannot understand how their pets managed to get together with a tom.

The explanation is that the cat only thinks it is having kittens, a condition known as false or pseudo-pregnancy. If it seems to be making the animal uncomfortable, the vet can prescribe a few hormone tablets. Less serious cases need only time and patience.

Birth

Before the kittens arrive, provide the queen with a choice of nesting sites. Cardboard boxes lined with paper towels are suitable because they can be changed easily and will not smother the kittens. The mother-to-be should be confined to the room with the chosen box once she starts having contractions.

The first stage of labour can extend for many hours. The cat is restless and will not eat, though she will drink from time to time. Eventually the second stage of labour commences – contractions – which may last up to six hours. The queen may also have a vaginal discharge, clear or cloudy water and some blood. The contractions gradually become stronger and more frequent, and prior to the expulsion of the first kitten, a sac of fluid may be passed, preparing the passage for the birth. Soon, she will bear down, and the first kitten will emerge. Kittens may be born head first or tail first, both presentations being equally normal. The head or rump appears, and the cat licks at the membranes as contractions push the tiny kitten out. Sometimes, particularly with the first born, the kitten seems to be held back by its shoulders or hips, but it is normally expelled without human interference as the cat shifts her position and bears down. She licks away all the membranes encasing the newly born kitten, and chews the umbilical cord to within about 2 cm (½ in) of the kitten's body. The stump of cord dries and drops off, leaving a neat navel within about a week. The placenta may be passed still attached to the kitten, or may be expelled later, after the kitten is clean, dry and nursing. The mother cat will normally eat the placenta, which is rich in nutrients, and which, in the wild, would sustain her until she was fit enough to hunt for food.

After the birth of the first kitten, the rest of the litter follow at regular or irregular intervals and the mother cat deals with each in the same way. She licks and washes each kitten, clearing the membrane from its body, cleaning the mucus from its nose and mouth and stimulating it to breathe. She also licks vigorously at the kitten's anal region, stimulating the tiny animal to pass the meconium, a dark plug which stops up its bowel until released.

Each kitten will be born separately, with its own membranes and placenta. The time between each kitten can be as little as a few minutes or as long as several hours. Most litters consist of four or five kittens. To determine which are male or female at this early stage, note that females generally have less space between the anal hole and the genitals than males.

Keep the mother away from tom cats until after the

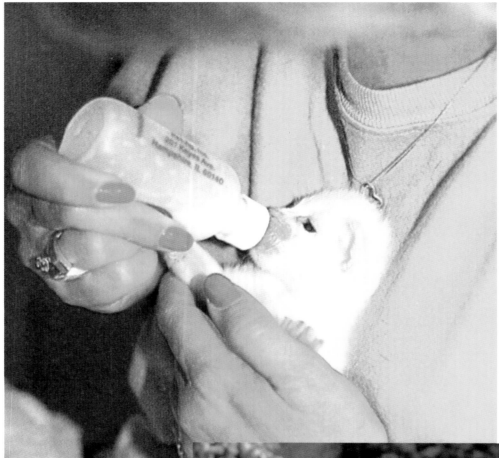

Left *A kitten will need its mother, or a substitute for the first five or six months. An orphaned kitten can be raised on a bottle.*

Right *Once her kittens are fully mobile, the mother cat encourages them to explore and broaden their play and hunting behaviours.*

kittens have been weaned because she may come into oestrus within a few days of giving birth and conceive again. A series of close-together pregnancies is likely to damage her health.

When the last kitten of the litter has been born, the mother cat washes her own genital region, legs and tail. She gathers her kittens together and lying on one side, encourages them to suckle. She may not leave the nest for up to 24 hours for food and a drink.

She has a set routine for kitten care. After nursing the kittens, she washes and grooms them in turn, and swallows all the excreted material they produce, to ensure that the nest remains clean. This would be a safety factor in the wild, preventing scent leaving clues as to the kittens' whereabouts and thus attracting predators.

At birth, the kittens should be approximately 13 cm (5 in) long and weigh between 60 and 140 g (2 and 5 oz). Because they are born with eyes closed and ears folded, they cannot see or hear. Therefore, their senses of smell and touch are vital in satisfying their needs for food and warmth. Although breeds differ, cats are approximately the equivalent of two to three human years old at three months of age, and reach about 46 cm (18 in) at the end of their first year. Then they age gradually, several equivalent human years every year, and are approximately 25 after two years, 30 after three years, 40 after five years, 50 after eight years and 60 after ten years.

While they are still kittens, the mother communicates vocally at first, using various noises for scolding, greeting, enticing and warning. Later on, visual signals also become important. For example, the mother uses her tail to lead them. Even after centuries of domestication, cats often revert to the innate behaviour patterns of their wild forebears. Three weeks or so after the birth of her litter, the cat may suddenly decide to move the kittens to another, often quite unsuitable,

Right The mother cat constantly grooms her kittens, washing them by licking them all over with her rough tongue.

Right A mother cat may decide to move her litter to a new nest and carries the kittens one at a time, holding them firmly by the scruff of the neck.

location. She grasps each kitten round the neck, holding it in her jaws, but not piercing the skin with her teeth, then lifts the kitten by raising her head and carries it between her straddled forelegs to its new resting place. The cat will carry each kitten in turn until she is satisfied that the litter is in a new, safe haven. When kittens are grasped around the neck, their natural response is to assume the foetal position and go completely limp. This ensures that they are rarely harmed by being carried by their mother.

Kittens may instinctively hiss or spit if disturbed, even before their eyes open. Another protective habit is to bed down with their siblings, both for warmth and to keep the litter together.

Until the kittens are about three weeks old, the

Right If your litter are pedigrees, about the fifth week they should be registered as such with one of the cat fancy associations. The certificate validates cats as authentic members of a particular breed by listing from four to seven generations of forebears.

mother cat looks after all their needs. She leaves the litter only for short periods to eat, drink and relieve herself, and returns as quickly as possible to her babies. By ten days, the kittens have opened their eyes and gradually begin to respond to various stimulae. During their third and fourth weeks, they try to leave the nest area, and as they become stronger and more mobile, and gradually accept solid food, the mother spends less time with them. This timing will vary between different breeds, and indeed between individual kittens. Litter training can be started during the third week, and the kittens will start to wash themselves, play and hunt soon after.

By about the fifth week, they should be registered as pedigrees with one of the cat fancy associations. The certificate validates cats as authentic members of a particular breed by listing from four to seven generations of forebears.

Veterinary care should begin in the ninth week, with initial vaccinations; another vaccination at 12 weeks, followed by spaying (female) or neutering (male) at 16 weeks and 36 weeks respectively.

Although kittens can leave the nest after six weeks, they will not be totally independent of the mother (or a substitute) for another five months.

Development of kittens

Kittens are born blind and deaf. They have a strong sense of smell, however, which enables them to locate their mother's nipples, and a strong sucking reflex which ensures that they take in enough milk to satisfy their needs. At about one week to ten days after birth, the eyes open and the hearing starts to develop, and until the litter is three weeks of age the queen looks after the kittens constantly, feeding and grooming them and stimulating them to urinate and defecate by licking at their genital regions. The queen ingests the kittens' wastes at this time and spends about 70 per cent of her time curled up with, and attending to, her family.

At two weeks the kittens can scrabble around their nest box and at three weeks start to stand up on their legs and pay attention to what is going on around them. Between three and six weeks they make great advances, learning to play, to make sounds, and show an interest in solid food. From about four weeks they will use a corner of their box for toilet purposes and by six weeks can be taught to use a litter tray. Having learned to eat a variety of foods and to spend less time with their mother, most kittens are fully independent and self-sufficient by about eight to ten weeks of age.

Newborn

One week

Two weeks

Three weeks

Six weeks

THE THINKING CAT

The mature cat displays all those qualities of independence and self-sufficiency that its human family finds so compelling.

It spends less time playing and more time in activities that have a clearly defined purpose. With adulthood, the cat gains confidence and tends to fall into an ordered routine of day-to-day living. It accommodates itself to its household's way of life and the limitations of territory.

Cats gradually get to know their neighbours and they evolve a social order. One male cat will wait for another to pass. This could be a recognition of territorial rights; it could also be a sign of respect for superior strength.

Cats recognize and tolerate those that they know. Strangers are fought off. They soon learn that the fat, old King Charles Spaniel next door can be safely and completely ignored. The nasty little terrier across the street, however, must be kept in a state of constant fear. Each and every time it shows its face it must be met by a formidable display of ruffled fur, enlarged tail and a threatening hiss.

The cat has acquired skills and techniques in order to adapt to its environment. As well as protecting itself and its territory the cat now hunts. The first step, of course, is to gain access to the hunting grounds. This poses no problem for farmyard cats or their feral cousins. But the hearthside cat may have to wait patiently by the door to the basement or garden for several hours until it is given the opportunity to make a furtive dash to begin an expedition.

Cats learn in kittenhood that certain actions result in either reward or punishment. Some are particularly quick to learn that by swinging on door handles, for instance, doors open, making hunting grounds more easily accessible.

The mature cat may take control of its own existence. Many are the tales of cats being fed in more than one household, exacting affection and attention wherever they go. The family with which a cat normally lives will be greatly concerned when the pet stays away from home for more than 24 hours. It may have been in some difficulties, but more often it is exercising that independence which is so attractive. A feline assignation or an equally warm fire elsewhere, a moonlight hunting trip or extra-rich morsels from a neighbour's table are just some of the possible excuses which it might give.

THE CLEAN CAT

Many people choose to keep a cat because they believe it to be fastidious and clean in its personal toilet habits. This is certainly true of most cats, and the reason may be, as some experts have suggested, that they simply cannot stand any sort of mess around them.

Left *The cat licks a paw then uses it to wash one the side of its face, then changes to the other paw and washes the other side.*

They do not even like using a dirty litter tray, but will do so if they are unable to go out. One can only guess at the reasons for the cat's behaviour in burying its own body waste but, as with most animals, the pattern is predetermined, and seldom varies from that of its ancestors, no matter how remote they are in the evolutionary chain.

The most obvious reason for the burying ritual is that the cat wishes to avoid leaving telltale signs that could lead an enemy to the nest. However, just to underline how perverse they can be, cats sometimes do it not for concealment, but for territorial marking.

The cat may also feel that in burying its excrement, it is reducing the chances of itself, its young or its extended family, being re-infested by its own internal parasites. However, it may be deluding itself, for with increased urbanization and domestication, in addition to smaller toilet areas, the opposite could happen. The worms and their eggs become concentrated in a very small area and the cat is, in fact, cultivating a garden of parasites injurious to itself.

Another reason for the behaviour may be the certain amount of satisfaction involved in following a ritual, no matter what the purpose, and there may be frustration if it is curtailed or hurried in any way.

While the mother cat is nursing her young, she keeps the nest clean by the simple expedient of swallowing everything they leave behind. However repugnant to humans, this practice must have evolved because no rational alternative was available.

Cats will be cats, whether in town or country. The urban animal will dig into a litter tray, made of plastic or steel, in exactly the same manner as its country cousins dig into loam. Like a programmed computer, it cannot stop itself.

CLIMBING EQUIPMENT

A sheathed knife stays sharp. That is the reason why cats retract their claws. They must keep them razor-sharp to meet every contingency, for these controllable extensions of the body are essential.

In contrast, the claws of a dog are more like finger nails. They may add protection to the digits, but hardly compare with the sensitive functions of a cat's claws.

There is no point in cutting or blunting the claws because you think them too sharp. The cat knows what it needs and will head straight for the nearest tree-trunk and restore the points. You cannot change a million years of evolution with a few snips of the scissors.

How do cats climb? They use the hind legs to propel themselves neatly and apparently effortlessly as far as possible, and then they scramble. If an irate enemy is in hot pursuit, this initial leap and scramble may carry the cat anything up to about 3.5m (12ft).

How do you get a cat out of a tree? The easiest way is to drag it down, but this will entail a few scratches. The best way is simply to do nothing and wait. After a few hours, the panic will subside and the cat will begin the process of inching its way down again.

Right Climbing is part of a cat's way of life, but to do it efficiently, sharp claws are a must. These fully-controllable extensions enable the animal to gain a firm foothold in the most unlikely places. How do you get a cat out of a tree? The easiest way is to drag it down, but this will entail a few scratches. The best way is simply to do nothing and wait. After a few hours, the panic will subside and the cat will begin the process of inching its way down again.

CAN CATS REMEMBER?

You may want your cat to remember that you don't want it to scratch the furniture. Or lie on your favourite black sweater. Or bring prey back to the house. You have made these requests clear to your cat time and again. And you are sure that if your cat had any capacity at all for memory it would remember these few simple rules. Wouldn't it?

Not necessarily. Cats have a great capacity for learning and memory, but they tend to save it for useful information – useful to them – and for their own gain or comfort not yours. Cats remember what they like to eat and the location of their water dish; how to find a litter box and how to use it; the look, sound and feel of their favourite toy (or toys) and where those objects are at any given moment; the taste of their favourite prey and the best location for stalking it; what to do when they tire, and the location of the sunniest, warmest, cosiest sleeping spot in the house.

They remember which of the noises they make are effective in getting their owners to respond to their various wants, and usually at mealtimes they remember their own names. Outside, they remember the location of their territory and that of other cats, and what things in the neighbourhood to avoid – like puddles and dogs, in some cases. But their memory is selective, and only with proper training will they 'remember' things you want them to know.

Aside from the mundane, some cats are known to have extraordinary 'memories' for finding places. Taken away from their homes, they are able to remember where they live. (This doesn't work if a family moves, leaving the cat behind. The cat tracks down the place, not the people.)

The key to this homing ability is built-in celestial navigation, similar to that used by birds. During the time a cat lives in a particular house its brain automatically registers the angle of the sun at certain times of the day. Should a cat leave or be taken away

***Left** Cats have a great capacity for learning and memory, but they tend to save it for useful information. Cats remember what they like to eat and the location of their water dish and the sound of the can opener.*

from that house, it can find it again by using its internal biological clocks, through trial and error, to put the angle of the sun in the right place. It doesn't even need a clear day to navigate; it uses polarized light. This homing ability has also been attributed to cats' sensitivity to the Earth's magnetic fields. When magnets are attached to cats, their normal navigational skills are disrupted. Such navigation occurs in the subconscious, but eventually the cat finds itself in a neighbourhood that smells, looks and sounds like its old area.

Cats can also remember people and animals they come into contact with. They will recognize who treats them well and who mistreats them. But, alas, a mother cat that meets up with one of her kittens later in life is not likely, or at least does not show the ability, to remember it as a creature she once carried inside her and fed.

Your cat's daily routine probably coincides with and, in some cases, depends on, your schedule. It awakens when you do, goes to bed when you do, eats when you provide food, and goes out when you decide it's time. As it learns your routine, it picks up on pre-routine signals, especially when the payoff is food or warmth.

Does your cat jump up on your bed to snuggle in for the night when it sees or hears you get into bed? Or is it already there when you turn in, having heard you turn off the TV or run the water to brush your teeth?

Does it come running when it hears the can opener? Or does it anticipate breakfast when you turn on the coffee-maker or emerge from the shower?

Below *Cats have a memory for things important to their lives, such as a prime mousing location.*

Vocal cords

The vocal apparatus of cats is very different from that of humans. Vocal sounds are produced by changes in the tension of muscles in the throat and mouth, and by changes in the speed of air moving over the vocal cords, which are stretched across the larynx. The vibration of the 'false' vocal cords may be involved in purring.

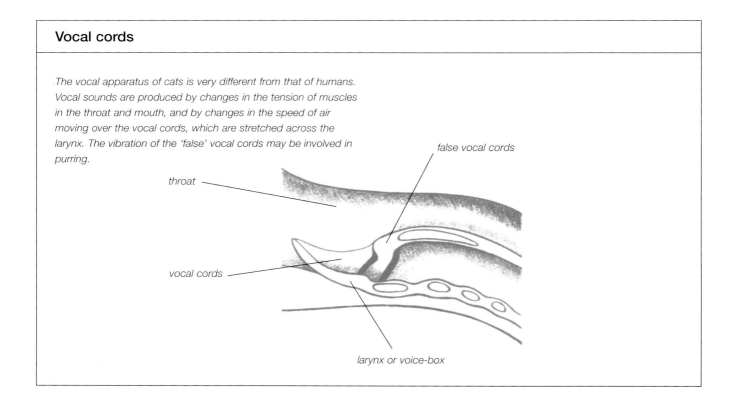

false vocal cords

throat

vocal cords

larynx or voice-box

of soothing potential aggressors, proving that purring should not be taken as a sign of good health.

Miaowing, another sound readily associated with cats, is often the call of an abandoned or unhappy kitten – if they are cold, lost, awakened by a returning mother, or in some other way annoyed and malcontent. Adult cats also miaow to signal discontent, unhappiness or need, perhaps even a need for mating. Cats of both sexes use a version of miaowing for a mating call.

Gurgling, a high-pitched, friendly greeting, is less common. If combined with gentle meows, it becomes a kind of social contact sound known as 'chatting'. Although it varies from one cat to another, some cats will do it for half an hour or more and modulate sound so much that they rarely repeat themselves. Another version of gurgling occurs when a mother first brings prey to her kittens. Gurgling can also border on a scream when mum is announcing prey that is larger and possibly dangerous.

Screeching is what cats do when they are in great distress; it is also done just after mating.

Anyone who has ever heard a cat in the night knows the crying sound of a tom cat caterwauling. The call is usually mistaken for a love song, but it is actually a cry of threat and war. Toms rivalling for the same queen are especially known to threaten each other with caterwauling.

Hissing is an audible warning sign that is made when cats expel their breath hard. They expel it so hard when hissing that if one is close enough he or she can feel the air jet. That's why cats shy away if you blow in their faces; even the look of hissing without sounds or air movement can repulse cats.

Growling is an offensive, rather than defensive, sound. Repeated growling turns into snarling.

Tooth-chattering occurs when cats see prey but cannot reach it. Because they want the prey so badly, they move their mouths as if they were in the process of killing.

CAT NAPPING

Whereas human beings spend about a third of their lives asleep, the cat averages more than 60 per cent.

Scientists do not know the causes or the functions of sleep but they do know that prolonged interruptions of the cycle of rest periods can produce illness. They also differentiate between five different kinds, ranging from a light, sensory drift or 'floating', through light sleep to three degrees of deep sleep. The first is the phenomenon of catnapping, which is so well recognized that the term describes that form of human sleep.

Many cats choose old trophies or half-open drawers to sleep in, along with the traditional spot on the family armchair. This is because, unlike dogs which flop down anywhere, cats need security before sleeping. Some exotic fish secrete a cocoon around themselves before they go to sleep; the cat will go to considerable lengths in order to emulate this, using objects in the domestic environment to achieve it. This does not apply to catnapping, when any perch will do.

Many sedative drugs can alter the character of paradoxical sleep and cats appear to be more sensitive to these drugs than other domesticated animals. They should be used only when absolutely necessary. Perhaps the sleep they induce changes dreams into nightmares.

Below *Cats need to feel secure before adopting this sleeping position, unlike catnapping when any perch will do.*

Below and right *The leisurely ritual of yawning and stretching; these yoga-like exercises are performed to restore circulation after sleep.*

WAKING UP

Home-bound cats often follow the routine of the people with whom they live. Despite the seasons and the weather, alarm clocks ring and activities begin at the same hour each day. The cat soon learns that all this jangling activity is the prelude to its breakfast. That is, for five days of the week.

But there may be two days of the week that this frantic bustle does not happen. No matter how hungry, or how piteously it miaows for its breakfast, the whole ritual is postponed for no clearly decipherable reason. The mature cat knows that it might just as well roll over and go back to sleep.

A common definition of sleep is that it is that state in which activity and interaction with the outside world decrease or indeed stop altogether. The obvious bodily changes that take place are that both the heart and respiratory rate become considerably slower. Some animals sleep so deeply during hibernation that it is not always possible to tell, even with the aid of a stethoscope, that the heart is beating.

Many a child has brought a 'dead' tortoise, hamster or hedgehog to the vet for disposal only to be assured that it is only sleeping very deeply. At the other end of the scale, there are animals like antelopes that hardly sleep at all.

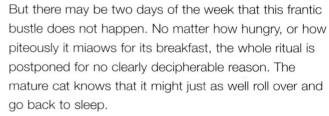

They have to be ready to escape at all times. Some animals remain vigilant while others in their community rest. The swift manages the clever trick of sleeping while flying – during gliding it can catch the occasional nap.

The temperature of the body drops slightly in warm-blooded animals. Bats become almost cold-blooded during sleep. When they wake they must stretch and exercise to raise their temperature to a normal level. Similarly, the waking cat (if it has not been startled) will go through a leisurely ritual of yawning and stretching. These yoga-like exercises are performed with a thoroughness that relatively stiff-muscled humans envy and try to emulate. Every single joint from the top of the head to the tip of the tail appears to be moved. This has the function of restoring full circulation and instant readiness for action to every part of the body. It may also be one of the ways in which an apparently sedentary creature keeps itself superbly fit.

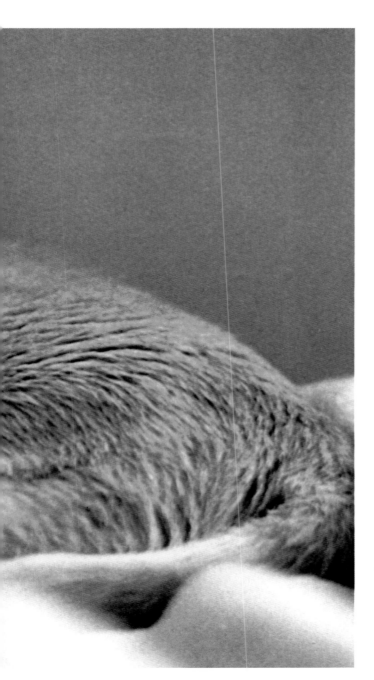

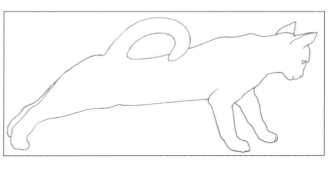

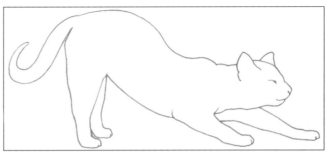

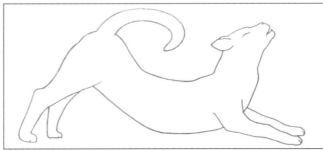

Above left and right *Most humans make do with one all-embracing stretch. Cats usually embark on a whole series of movements, designed to loosen almost every area in the most pleasant and satisfying manner. This process is presented as a public performance, unlike so many feline activities, and it will usually commence with a joint and muscle-loosening extension of the front legs. No respecters of such trifles as your upholstery or carpets, cats will dig their claws in to give themselves an effective*

anchorage. This is followed by the arching of the back, in which the animal squeezes itself into an amazing and concertina-like posture, before completing the acrobatic and, at times, almost balletic spectacle. The finale is usually reserved for the rear legs, which are each stretched out in turn. The whole show can be accompanied by a further selection of face-twisting yawns. When this ritual is over the self-respecting cat feels able to face the world.

CAT CARE

The domestic cat is quite easy to care for within the confines of the home. It must be provided with some basic equipment, such as feeding and drinking bowls, a comfortable bed, a litter tray and scratching post.

Keeping your cat healthy is mainly a matter of common-sense and proper husbandry. In the first place, the cat needs to have been properly reared as a kitten, and should be regularly vaccinated against the most dangerous feline diseases such as panleukopaenia, or infectious enteritis, rhinotracheitis and calicivirus, often called cat 'flu, and feline leukaemia virus. All cats should be fed a well-balanced diet, and receive regular courses of anthelmintics to ensure that they are free from internal parasites. External parasites such as fleas should be controlled by the application of pest powder or sprays when necessary, or by dosing with a product designed to curtail the fleas' breeding cycle. The cat's toilet tray must be maintained in spotless condition at all times as must its food and water bowls.

Given such care, and lots of love and attention, the cat should always remain in good health.

A vast range of equipment is available for the comfort of the pet cat, and in a broad price band.
Right *Disposable cardboard carrier, soft and padded sleep-igloo, water and food dish, soft toy.*
Top Right *A pure bristle grooming brush, non-toxic, unbreakable toys and a litter tray.*

Below The length of a cat's life varies enormously. Those living wild as strays may only survive for two years or so, while a cherished pet may live well into its teens, an old age pensioner in human terms.

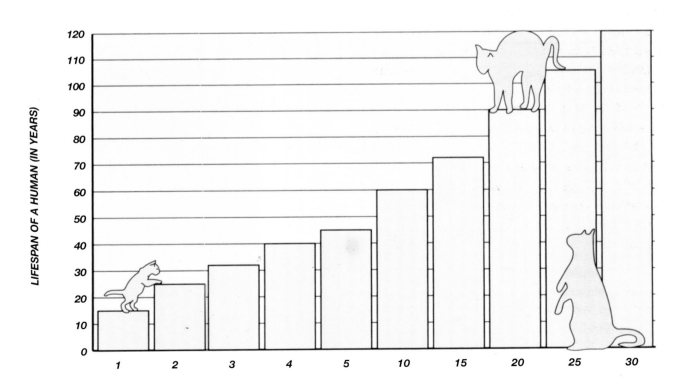

LIFESPAN OF A CAT (IN YEARS)

CAT ORGANIZATIONS

The following is a list of the main cat fancy organizations throughout the world.

American Cat Association, Inc.
8101 Katherine Ave
Panorama City, CA 91402, USA

American Cat Fanciers' Association (ACFA)
PO Box 203
Point Lookout, MO 65726, USA

American Feline Society
41 Union Square W
New York, NY 10003, USA

American Humane Association
5351 S Roslyn St
Englewood, CO 80111, USA

American Society for the Prevention of Cruelty to Animals
441 E 92nd St, New York, NY 10028, USA

Canadian Cat Association (CCA)
14 Nelson St W, Suite 5
Brampton, Ontario, L6X 1BY, Canada

Canadian Society for the Prevention of Cruelty to Animals
5214 Jean-Talon St W
Montreal, Quebec, H4P 1X4, Canada

Cat Fanciers' Association (CFA)
PO Box 430
Red Bank, NJ 07701, USA

The Cat Fanciers' Club of South Africa
PO Box 783100
Sandton, 2146, SOUTH AFRICA

Cat Fanciers' Federation
2013 Elizabeth St
Schenectady, NY 12303, USA

Cat Survival Trust
Marlind Centre
Codicote Road
Welwyn, Hertfordshire, AL6 9TV, UK

Cats Protection League
20 North St
Horsham, West Sussex, RH12 1BN, UK

Co-ordinating Cat Council of Australia (CCC of A)
GPO Box 4317
Sydney, NSW 2001, AUSTRALIA

Crown Cat Fanciers' Association
1379 Tyler Park Drive
Louisville, KY 40204, USA

Kensington Kitten and Neuter Cat Club
Fairmont
78 Highfield Ave
Aldershot, Hampshire, UK

Long Island Ocelot Club
PO Box 99542
Tacoma, WA 98499, USA

National Cat Club
The Laurels
Chesham Lane
Wendover, Buckinghamshire, UK

Royal Society for the Prevention of Cruelty to Animals
(RSPCA)
Wilberforce Way
Southwater
Horsham, West Sussex, RH13 9RS, UK

United Cat Federation
6621 Thornwood St
San Diego, CA 92111, USA

Fédération Internationale Feline (FIFe)
23 Doerhavelaan
Eindhoven, 5644 BB, NETHERLANDS

Feline Advisory Bureau
350 Upper Richmond Road
Putney, London, SW15 6TL, UK

Governing Council of the Associated Cat Clubs of
South Africa
45 Edison Drive
Meadowridge, 7800, SOUTH AFRICA

Governing Council of the Cat Fancy (GCCF)
4–6 Penel Orlieu
Bridgwater, Somerset, TA6 3PG, UK

The International Cat Association (TICA)
PO Box 2684
Harlingen, TX 78551, USA

GLOSSARY

Abscess A localized collection of pus in part of the body, formed by tissue disintegration and surrounded by an inflamed area. In cats, these are commonly the result of bites or scratches occurring from fighting and, if left untreated, can be fatal.

Abyssinian An Oriental shorthair with a distinctly ticked tawny coat.

Acinonyx A genus of *Felidae* including only one species, the cheetah.

Acute Metritis An infection of the uterus.

Agouti In a Tabby cat, the colour between the stripes.

Balinese A breed of Oriental cat with long hair and Siamese-style markings.

Banding Individual bands of colour growing in a cross-wise direction.

Bengal Cat A very large breed of cat with either spots or marbled patterns on their coats.

Bib The lengthened hair around the chest area; part of the ruff.

Bi-colour A cat with a patched coat of white and a second colour.

Birman A semi-longhaired colour-point domesticated cat with a pale cream coloured body and coloured gloves of seal, blue, chocolate, lilac, lynx and red.

Calicivirus A serious respiratory disease.

Calico A coat pattern that is mottled in tones of black, orange and white.

California Spangled Cat A large, strong, spotted cat with a somewhat wild appearance as they were bred to look like a small leopard.

Calling A term used to describe a female cat's behaviour (i.e. howling, yowling, screaming) during ovulation.

Cameo-Chinchilla A coat that is shaded or smoked with red or cream tipping.

Cardiomyopathy A disease or disorder of the heart muscle, especially of unknown or obscure cause.

Carpal Pads The pads on the wrists of a cat's front legs which provide traction.

Dam The female parent.

Dander Small scales from the skin, hair or feathers of an animal, often causing an allergic reaction in sensitive individuals.

Declawing A surgical procedure to permanently remove the claws.

Dehydration Excessive loss of water from the body or from an organ or body part, as from illness or fluid deprivation.

Devon Rex Cat A breed of cat with a sparse, curly, very soft coat.

Ear Mites Microscopic insects that survive by feeding on the lining of the ear canal.

Egyptian Mau Cat A medium-sized shorthair cat breed with a naturally spotted coat.

Elizabethan Collar A type of hood in the shape of a cone which is worn around the neck to keep animals from irritating an injury.

Entire A cat whose reproductive system is complete or has not been altered.

FCV Acronym for Feline Calcivirus, a virus that causes upper respiratory disease

Feline Of or belonging to the family *Felidae*, which includes the lions, tigers, jaguars and wild and domestic cats.

Feline Immunodeficiency Virus A virus which invades a cat's DNA and ultimately causes dysfunction of the immune system.

Feline Leukaemia Virus A group of diseases commonly causing cancer and death.

Feral Having returned to an untamed state from domestication.

Feral-Domestic Hybrid A hybrid between a wild cat species and a domestic cat.

Gastric Of, relating to, or associated with the stomach.

Gastritis Chronic or acute inflammation of the stomach, especially of the mucous membrane of the stomach.

Genealogy Recorded family descent.

Genotype The genetic makeup, as distinguished from the physical appearance, of an organism or a group of organisms.

Habit A recurrent, often unconscious pattern of behaviour that is acquired through frequent repetition.

Half-Pedigree A term referring to a cat with one pedigree parent. In the strictest terms, however, a half-pedigree is still considered a mixed breed.

Hand-Feed The process of feeding a cat periodically throughout the day and for a limited time.

Havana Brown Cat A moderately sized, muscular shorthair cat with a brown or reddish-brown coat and green eyes.

Haw A nictitating membrane, especially of a domesticated animal.

Heat Seasonal period of the female. Oestrus, in season.

Haemorrhage Excessive discharge of blood from the blood vessels; profuse bleeding.

ICF Acronym for Independent Cat Federation.

Icteric Affected by jaundice which causes yellowing of the skin and the whites of the eyes, often caused by liver failure.

Idiopathic Of, relating to, or designating a disease having no known cause.

Immune Response The body's reaction to infection.

Immunization To produce immunity in, as by inoculation.

Innate Possessed at birth; inborn

Inbreeding The mating of two closely related cats of the same breed.

Infertile Not fertile; unproductive or barren.

Jacobsen's Organ A sense organ located in a cat's mouth that functions somewhere between smell and taste.

Japanese Bobtail Cat A breed of cat coming in both longhair and shorthair varieties.

Jowls Flesh of the lips and jaws.

Kennel Cough Tracheobronchitis of dogs or cats.

Kindle Term for a group of kittens.

Kink A bump, bend, twist or curl in the tail bone.

Kitten A young cat, typically below the age of 6 months.

Korat Cat A shorthair cat with a small to medium build appearing sleek and muscular.

Laces Term for the white markings on the legs.

Lactation Secretion or formation of milk by the mammary glands.

Laryngitis Inflammation of the larynx.

Lavender A pale, pinkish-gray colour to the coat. See also *Lilac*.

Lilac A pale, pinkish-gray colour to the coat. See also *Lavender*

Line Breeding The practice of mating a cat to a member of an earlier generation of the cat's bloodline.

Mackerel A term referring to a type of tabby pattern in which the colours of the coat appear striped.

Maine Coon Cat One of the largest breeds of domestic cat with very long dense fur and a bushy tail that is often striped. Native to North America.

Manx Cat A breed of cat with a naturally occurring mutation of the spine, leading to longer hind legs than front legs. Usually tailless, though some have a small stub of a tail.

Mask A term referring to the darker shadings on the face as seen in Siamese and Himalayans.

Microchip A rice-sized device encoded with a unique and unalterable number. The chip is implanted just under the skin in the scruff of the neck and is read by a scanner.

Nebelung Cat A longhaired cat bred to resemble the Russian Blue cat except with a long coat.

Necklace A term referring to the bandings of colour across the lower neck and chest area which give the appearance of a necklace.

Neuter Castration of a male cat.

Nictitating Membrane A transparent inner eyelid that closes to protect and moisten the eye. Also called third eyelid.

Norwegian Forest Cat A breed of domestic cat native to Northern Europe and characterized by a thick, fluffy double-layered coat, and a long bushy tail.

Ocicat A new breed of cat characterized by a coat with spots that resemble a wild cat.

Odd-Eyed Eyes of different colour, such as one brown eye and one blue eye.

Oestrus The periodic state of sexual excitement in the female cat that immediately precedes ovulation and during which the female is most receptive to mating.

Olfactory Of, relating to, or contributing to the sense of smell.

Onychectomy The medical term for declawing, the surgical removal of a cat's claws.

Panleukopaenia A viral infection that attacks the bones and intestinal walls, also known as Feline Infectious Enteritis (FIE).

Papers A cat's pedigree and registration slip.

Papillae Tiny, finger-like hooks found on a cat's tongue and lining the gut.

Parti-Colour A coat of two or more distinct colours.

Pedigree The written record of a cat's genealogy, often of three generations or more.

Queen A whole, unspayed female cat.

Quick The vein running through a cat's claw.

Rabies An acute, infectious, often fatal viral disease of most warm-blooded animals, especially wolves, cats, and dogs, that attacks the central nervous system and is transmitted by the bite of infected animals.

Ragdoll Cat A breed of longhaired cat with a sturdy body, short legs and a long thick coat with Siamese-style points.

Red A coat colour. Also known as orange, ginger or marmalade.

Registration A recording of a cat's birth, ancestry and other particulars with an official organization.

Sable A term referring to the colour black, the darkest coat colour in Burmese.

Scratching Post A tower-like structure typically covered in burlap allowing cats to safely scratch or rub their nails.

Scottish Fold Cat A breed of cat with a natural mutation to its ears with the ear cartilage containing a fold so the ears bend forwards and down towards the front of their head.

Seal A term referring to the dark brown colour found at the point of the darkest variety of Siamese.

Secondary Coat The fine hairs which make up the undercoat.

Self Also known as solid, a term used to describe a coat of a single, uniform colour.

Selkirk Rex Cat A breed of cat with highly curled hair, including the whiskers.

Semi-Feral A cat which, though not domesticated, still lives near and is accustomed to humans, such as barn cats.

Semi-Longhair A type of longhair cat without an extremely long coat, such as the Maine Coon.

Tabby A term referring to a coat pattern that consists of two or more colours in a striped pattern.

Tabby Tortoiseshell A term referring to a tortoiseshell coat that has tabby black patching.

Tapetum Lucidum The highly reflective portion of the interior of the cat's eyeball that aids in night vision.

Tapeworm Any of various ribbonlike, often very long flatworms of the class *Cestoda*.

Taurine An essential nutritional substance for cats which can help prevent blindness and certain types of heart disease.

Testicles The male gonads, which produce spermatoza.

UCF Acronym for the United Cat Federation.

Unaltered Term referring to a male or female cat who has not been neutered or spayed and has full reproductive abilities.

Undercoat The layer of the coat comprised of down hairs.

Undercolour A term referring to the colour of the hair closest to the skin.

Uterus A hollow muscular organ located in the pelvic cavity of female mammals in which the fertilized egg implants and develops.

Valerian: A plant whose scent is attractive to cats.

Van Pattern A term used to describe a bicolour coat consisting of a mostly white body with colour restricted to the extremities (head, tail, etc.)

Wean The process of making a kitten eat solid food instead of its mother's milk.

Whisker Break A term referring to an indentation in the upper jaw.

Whisker Pad A term referring to the thickened or fatty pads around the whisker area.

Whole Not neutered or spayed.

White Spotting A term referring to a coat pattern of random patches of white on a coloured coat which vary from small spots to large areas.

York Chocolate Cat A new American breed of show cat with a long, fluffy coat and a plumed tail.

Zoonosis A disease of animals, such as rabies or psittacosis, that can be transmitted to humans.

INDEX